YOUTH IN EGYPT

Youth in Egypt

Identity, Participation, and Opportunity

Nadine Sika

NEW YORK UNIVERSITY PRESS

New York

NEW YORK UNIVERSITY PRESS
New York
www.nyupress.org

References to Internet websites (URLs) were accurate at the time of writing. Neither the author nor New York University Press is responsible for URLs that may have expired or changed since the manuscript was prepared.

Please contact the Library of Congress for Cataloging-in-Publication data.

ISBN: 9781479819522 (hardback)
ISBN: 9781479819539 (paperback)
ISBN: 9781479819577 (library ebook)
ISBN: 9781479819560 (consumer ebook)

New York University Press books are printed on acid-free paper, and their binding materials are chosen for strength and durability. We strive to use environmentally responsible suppliers and materials to the greatest extent possible in publishing our books.

Manufactured in the United States of America

10 9 8 7 6 5 4 3 2 1

Also available as an ebook

To Mourad,

whose loving kindness and sense of humor

I shall carry with me forever

CONTENTS

Introduction

The political system that evolved in Egypt after the 1952 coup d'état is an interesting manifestation of the Dictator's Dilemma.[1] On the one hand, authoritarian rulers develop political strategies to acquire more political power, while on the other, they become more insecure through attaining it, leading to an increase in the repression and securitization that they impose on their society. In Egypt, over the years, this dilemma has been supported by a political economy that sustained authoritarian rule. Gamal Abdel Nasser established the Import Substitution and Industrialization (ISI) development model to change the social and class structure that preceded his rule.[2] Such a strategy was essential both for co-opting a large number of bureaucrats and for legitimizing and cementing Nasser's rule among a newly emerging social class. Collective action, however, was outlawed and coercion against political opponents was rampant. When Anwar Sadat came to power, he built on the authoritarian system already established by Nasser. However, he changed the ISI model to a market-oriented economy by partially liberalizing the political sphere and developing a market-oriented economy reliant on a new business elite. To achieve this, he co-opted both the economic elite and the new political elite, while in the meantime depending on the security apparatus, mainly the police force, to suppress his political opponents. Hosni Mubarak took Sadat's market-oriented economy even further, culminating in the adoption of a neoliberal economic model of sorts, in which state institutions became integrated into the privatization and reform processes.[3] He further built on Sadat's co-optation of the business elite and political opposition. The state security personnel were essential for repressing both the poor, who were most affected by the structural adjustment processes, and the political opposition. Abdel Fattah al-Sisi is further entrenching Mubarak's neoliberal model through other means. While the regime benefits from market liberalization and the elimination of state subsidies, the Egyptian military is deeply embedded in the market, developing its own industries and holding substantial stakes in the majority of infrastructure projects.[4] The security apparatus—the military and the police—has utilized repression against political opposition and subaltern groups who contest these reforms and are most affected by the elimination of subsidies.

During the past two decades, scholars have sought to understand the extent to which economic reforms based on structural adjustment programs and macroeconomic stabilization since Sadat's era have impacted the political structure. The major concern has been to ascertain how much state interventions, securitization, and crony capitalism have given rise to a neoliberal authoritarian regime. Other studies have analyzed the securitization of the polity and how neoliberalism has led to increased state repression, especially against the urban poor and the political opposition.[5] This book builds on these studies through demonstrating that the political economy of authoritarianism built by Nasser during the 1950s was fertile ground for the emergence of today's authoritarian political institutions in Egypt.[6] Concurrently, the economic liberalization policies first initiated by Sadat and extended by Mubarak have further deepened the authoritarian structure of the polity. This has led to a powerful amalgam of authoritarianism, securitization, and a locally adapted neoliberal system, a "cleft capitalist" system, or "Egypt's failed market making."[7]

These structural and neoliberal developments were not implemented in a vacuum, and they rapidly impacted citizens' daily lives and standards of living. Sometimes Egyptians resisted these structures through demonstrations and contestations. At other times they developed passive networks, where the "private encroachment of the ordinary" forced itself on the regime through incremental social changes.[8] The ouster of Mubarak in February 2011 marked a high moment of optimism regarding youth participation and protests against authoritarianism. However, this resistance was soon to fade with the inauguration of al-Sisi as president in 2014. The outcome of these daily struggles was little change: daily life remained within the confines of an authoritarian, securitized, neoliberal economic system.

This book examines the place and agency of youth in the contemporary phase of Egypt's political transformations, in the context of narrating and analyzing the relationships among political economy, authoritarianism, and citizens' daily struggles. What is the impact of the political economy of authoritarianism on young people in Egypt today? Who is more likely to be civically and politically engaged, and who is more likely to be marginalized from the formal economic, civic, and political spheres? Why and how do young people engage civically and politically within this system and why do others choose to exit?

To answer these questions, I utilize the political economy of youth approach, which is identified as

> a perspective that investigates the root causes and consequences of the positioning over time of the youth segment in relation to those (adults) in a given society with political and economic power. . . . In many societies, dominant political and economic power sources are closely aligned, and governments therefore have a tendency to develop policies favouring those with economic power, while ignoring or undermining the interests of those without economic power.[9]

The approach further "examines the extent to which the structural/materialist factors that position young people in society can also be related to the ideologies they accept."[10] It helps in examining and understanding what or who causes the different economic trends within a given society and who benefits or suffers from these same trends.[11] Mayssoun Sukarieh and Stuart Tannock, for instance, argue that youth studies have tended to understand how social, political, and economic contexts "frame and shape the lives of young people; only on occasion is consideration paid to the question of how young people and youth . . . play a role in shaping, organizing or legitimating social, cultural political and economic structures and practices."[12] Thus lies the importance of understanding youth agency within this macro structure.[13]

The political economy of youth approach mainly focuses on Western democratic regimes, and hence it does not analyze relations among neoliberalism, securitization, and authoritarianism in other parts of the globe. In this book, I link the political economy of youth approach to the current securitized, authoritarian political trends as well as the economic trends in Egypt, in order to understand who benefits or suffers within such a system. The complexity of this relation can be seen from what Lisa Wedeen argues is the contradictory logic of "neoliberal autocracy."[14] With that type of logic, an interest in market freedom is prevalent among citizens and rulers, to encourage upward mobility and developing economic advantages and opportunities, yet citizens' obedience to the repressive politics is in place.

This book demonstrates the complexity in which young people live today by outlining how they are impacted by the authoritarian, securitized, neoliberal system in which they live; how they deal with these challenges; and finally how, in the meantime, they become agents of change and continuity within the polity. I argue that the securitized, neoliberal system and the global neoliberal discourse have impacted both how young people perceive themselves and how they imagine change and reform to be. Some have chosen to be loyal through trying to reform the polity from within the formal sphere while others have chosen to voice their discontent through reforming the polity from outside the formal sphere; still others have chosen to exit through nonparticipation. One thing in common among all these variances of young people is that they do not want to overhaul the system, and their imagination for reform is within the boundaries of the global neoliberal discourse. Their major concerns and struggles are against corruption, nepotism, and repression.

The Liberal and the Securitized Perspectives of Youth

According to Karl Mannheim, people are exposed to the same social and historical stimuli, but they experience them differently based on their own social and economic status.[15] These experiences are stratified according to a person's generational location.[16] Younger generations experience historical events in a different manner from older generations. This difference is important for the development of social change within a polity.[17] According to Joseph Demartini, during times of rapid social and political change, generational conflicts develop. "Members of new generations often emerge as agents of change, both challenging traditional interpretations of historical conditions and offering alternative interpretations."[18] However, not all members of a generation manifest this conflictive relationship with others. Some agents for change are "generation units" composed of groups within the same "generation" who develop their common experiences in a different way from both older generations and their own generation.[19] Thus they can be at variance with their peers in the same generation.

Robert MacDonald argues that youth studies shed light on what the youth phase can tell us about a society at large. Research on youth expands our knowledge of the processes of social change and continuity, or social change and disruption.[20] When new social, economic, and political trends occur, these can be most clearly observed among newer generations. Another important reason for understanding youth is that we can analyze how powerful social actors, in particular the political elite in an authoritarian regime, try to develop narratives and policies about young people that in reality serve their own self-interest rather than that of youth.[21] Hence, analyzing the lives and interests of young people reveals the wider social and political transformations within a polity. The social construction of youth also reveals the political strategies of domination in authoritarian regimes.[22] In the context of the Arab world, Mark Tessler and his colleagues observed that different political generations are prevalent in various contexts in the region. Different age cohorts are influenced by varying historical situations and types of is-sues during certain periods within a country.[23]

The securitization of youth has become an important issue for analy-sis. Historically among policy makers there has been a dualism in refer-ring to young people.[24] This dualism has positioned youth within two dichotomous categories ". . . *youth as hope of the nation* against *youth as threat to social order.*"[25] Youth as hope, in this sense, is that young people constitute a force for socioeconomic development. They should be em-powered to achieve their main competencies to develop a productive society and economy.[26] In the developing world, especially in countries that have seen national struggles against colonialism in which young people have been the major dynamic behind nationalist movements, this dichotomy is extremely clear.[27] The potential of young people for social and political change entered the national liberation discourse, but it has been rapidly contained through various corporatist and authoritarian strategies.

While the positivist perspective to youth focuses on youth as *hope*, the securitization perspective to youth studies focuses on youth as *threat*.[28] When young people are perceived as a threat, their regimes and the in-ternational community see them as a liability and menace to the social order.[29] These two traditions have not addressed the impact of a global-ized neoliberal and authoritarian system on young people from disen-franchised backgrounds. These young people are the ones whom I refer to in the study as the *marginalized*. Marginalization here refers to a sys-tematic marginality that "results from disadvantages which people and communities experience in a socially constructed system of inequitable relations within a hegemonic order that allows one set of individuals and communities to exercise undue power and control over another set with the latter manifesting one or a number of vulnerability markers based on class, ethnicity, age, gender and other similar characteristics."[30] The gen-eral regime discourse toward these young people is that of exclusion and danger, which emanates from crime, and nondevelopment that is em-bedded in the urban informal settlements. They "grew up and worked in these areas and endured the effects of poor services, oversubscribed schools, public abuse, and government indifference."[31]

In the analysis for this book, I utilize these three categories (the hope, the threat, and the marginalized) intermittently. The first two categories are drawn from the literature to analyze how young people are perceived by their respective regimes, especially since the current regime in Egypt relies heavily on the securitization discourse while trying to accommodate youth to the developmental state-led youth initiatives.

Youth as an Age Cohort

Young people themselves, however, do not perceive themselves within the same categories as the regime does. For instance, some civically and politically engaged youth who work in "tolerated" organizations, like developmental nongovernmental organizations (NGOs), perceive themselves to be marginalized (see chapter 3). However, others within the same category perceive themselves as agents for change. Young people who are treated as a threat to the nation and to the social order by the regime believe that they are merely agents of positive change and development in society. The third category, the marginalized, contains those who are ignored by the state, while they themselves perceive that they are marginalized within the polity.

In their analysis of young people in the Middle East and North Africa (MENA) region, Michael Hoffman and Amaney Jamal argue that young people present a complicated age cohort. On the one hand, there are some commonalities and common intuitions among youth that are confirmed through the Arab Barometer survey. For instance, young people are less religious, more educated, more likely to protest, less likely to vote, and more likely to be unemployed than other age cohorts. On the other hand, they are more conservative, support political Islam more than older generations, and are more optimistic about the future.[32] The fieldwork on which this book relies adds to the research on youth cohorts through analyzing the variances within this age cohort.

The ways in which different young people react to state strategies present interesting insights to our understanding of state–society relations. The fieldwork shows that even though young people compose the same age cohort, they are not a single category and do not all share the same grievances and interests. They do indeed represent different "units," as Mannheim observes. Their reactions to state power and policies depend largely on their social, economic, and gender backgrounds. Some youth accept the political economy of authoritarianism and become tied to a network of patronage and are bound to become included within this structure. These young people accept the status quo, develop the same discourse as that of public officials, and assist in maintaining the vicious cycle of an authoritarian political economy. They believe the actions that are undertaken by the political and economic elites to justify the inequalities present in the polity. This serves the regime well, since these young people act "as social control mechanisms that stifle potential dissent that would otherwise threaten the hegemony of [neoliberal] capitalist ideologies."[33]

Other young people are convinced of the imminent need for reforming the economic, social, and political structures of the polity, yet they believe in reform from within, rather than revolting against the system. Accordingly, they become members of mainstream civil society organizations, develop economic and social initiatives that are tolerated by the regime, and bring about change one step at a time. They present what Albert Hirschman identifies as "loyalty."[34] These are youth who are loyal to the system and who feel an attachment to the regime and its institutions of which they believe themselves to be members. This sense of attachment and loyalty enables them to remain within the confines of an institution for a while, in the belief that reform will eventuate.

There are yet other young people who struggle against the authoritarian political economy and are thereby perceived as a threat to the nation. They develop different types of dissenting activities, from participating in protest movements to becoming independent activists standing against the regime. These young people are whom Hirschman describes as "voice"—they believe that the only way to reform the system is to voice their criticism against it.[35] They manifest the resistance to the manufacture of elite consent within Egypt, and they act in different ways through destabilizing the ideological arrangements that support the economic and political elite.[36] When these young people face socio-economic grievances, they can mobilize for collective political action against the regime.[37]

Poor and marginalized young people are from disenfranchised family backgrounds and are aware of the problems facing their nation: they prefer to exit rather than to voice their discontent, and to find parallel institutions and work in informal economies. This book demonstrates that these categories can be fluid, and some young people can at times move from loyalty to voice, from loyalty to exit, or from exit to voice.

All these young people, however, share one common identity, which is that of "youthfulness." They are linked together in "passive networks" through perceiving their common ways of living, common fashion, and common "pursuit of public fun."[38]

Youth and State–Society Relations

Beyond the enthusiasm raised by the recent wave of protests in the Arab world, largely perceived to be youth-led, Sukarieh and Tannock argue that the idea of youth as agents of change is not new.[39] Researchers in Western countries have analyzed this age cohort for centuries. However, in-depth analyses on the role of youth and student movements in perpetuating social, economic, and political change have only gained ground since the mid-twentieth century, prompted especially by the rising tide of youth activism in the United States during the mid-1960s. The role of young people in altering state–society relations has been at the center of much research in the past decade. Policy makers as well have been concerned with the role of youth both as "problems" and as "positive agents" for social change. However, to understand the importance of youth in their respective polities, and their influence on global society in general, we must analyze the context in which these young people live.

> This is not just because of the wide range of social and political actors involved in shaping the meaning and salience of youth, but also because of the extended scope of referents the concept of youth implicates. . . . Invocations about youth are often made in the context of social struggles and political agendas whose central concerns may only be symbolically or indirectly connected to the lives of individual young people.[40]

Recent developments in the region have shown that youth can have a major impact on the political, economic, social, and cultural spheres through conventional means, such as participating in mainstream civil society organizations, or unconventional means, especially through activism, protests, and youth-led economic and social initiatives.[41] Since their role in the spark of the Arab uprisings in 2010 and 2011, young people have developed new youth initiatives and movements that have crossed several red lines.[42] Young people have become the focus of public policy yet again with a second wave of Arab uprisings in 2018, which erupted in different countries, like Sudan, Algeria, and Lebanon.

Important as these unconventional methods are in highlighting the issue of youth participation, participation and activism should not be viewed only from a progressive perspective. In fact, youth activism might also lead to an opposite result—a further institutionalization of authoritarianism and neoliberalism.[43] For instance, the majority of NGOs in Egypt under Mubarak aligned themselves with the discourse of major international donors like USAID; at the same time, they were co-opted within the authoritarian structure to advance socioeconomic development without questioning the legitimacy of this system.[44] In Lebanon, civil society organizations have been important in institutionalizing the sectarian political system, through reinforcing the power of the political elite within each sect.[45] In Turkey and Egypt, young people belonging to the AKP (Justice and Development Party) in the first instance and to the Mostaqbal Watan Party (Nation's Future Party) in the second are examples of youth who work for the institutionalization of the status quo.[46]

Civic and political participation not only can occur as a form of contention against authoritarian regimes; it also can include collective action within the confines and even in support of those very regimes.[47] In early twentieth-century Europe, youth were linked and affiliated with conservative organizations. Those who belonged to different organizational structures, such as churches, political parties, or school unions, were also closely connected to the dominant political forces in their societies.[48] These young people have had a positive impact on the persistent social and political problems associated with nationalism and imperialism in their respective countries.[49] In the MENA region, young people who are part of the major established NGOs are more welcomed in the political sphere. Nevertheless, they strengthen the authoritarian structures in society by legitimating the regime. They promote the discourse that the regime tolerates the existence of civil society actors. For them, being allied to the regime with its corruption and authoritarian structure is a calculated decision to advance their own social, economic, and political objectives.[50] It is therefore no surprise that Arab governments, especially those in the middle- and lower-ranked economies like Egypt, Morocco, Tunisia, Jordan, and Lebanon, have favored civil society organizations that promote social services that can help to fill the social and economic gaps in education, healthcare, and welfare that the government is unable to fill. However, civil society organizations that promote human rights or support political participation have consistently been marginalized.[51] Funding sources for NGOs are highly restricted and must first be approved by governments. Ministries of the interior have the right to investigate the backgrounds of staff of civil society organizations. In Gaza, for instance, civil society organizations have to submit the personal biographies of their founding members to the Hamas-controlled Ministry of the Interior.[52]

Research Methods and Outline of the Book

This book relies heavily on quantitative and qualitative analysis of young people through fieldwork that was conducted in Egypt between April 2015 and April 2016. This was part of a larger three-year research project entitled Power2Youth (P2Y), which was carried out in six southeastern Mediterranean countries: Egypt, Lebanon, Morocco, Tunisia, Turkey, and the Palestinian Territories.[53] Qualitative field research was conducted prior to the quantitative field research for all countries. The qualitative research analyzed the extent to which young people who are members of political parties, social movements, youth initiatives, networks, trade unions, and charity organizations advance sociopolitical and economic change within their respective regimes.[54]

The book's six chapters, in addition to the introduction and conclusion, are based on the political economy of youth approach, which studies the origins of youth political positioning in their respective societies. It attempts to understand young people in Egypt, in relation to the "totality of social relations."[55] How do youth play a role in developing, contesting, and legitimating the polity? This will shed light on how the political economy of authoritarianism impacts the agency of young people and their role in social continuity and change in Egypt's ongoing political transformation. The book builds on the political economy of youth approach, which is not narrowly focused on young people per se but rather analyzes the changing nature of young people, as a social category in relation to the broader contexts of neoliberalism (cleft capitalism), securitization, and authoritarianism in Egypt. I take into account the "activities and agendas of a wide range of social actors."[56] I also consider the understanding of different interests of a large number of actors. It is important to look beyond young people within the polity, due to the fact that the meaning and positioning of youth in a polity can occur in different contexts of social and political struggles.[57] Thus, the first part of this book analyzes the totality of the political economy in Egypt, since the ascendancy of Nasser to power until the al-Sisi regime. Chapter 1 analyzes the historical background of the political economy of the authoritarian political system from Nasser until today. It discusses Nasser's role in establishing the "deep state." It then analyzes Sadat's extension of the authoritarian system to accommodate his market-oriented economy, as well as the intensification of the authoritarian, neoliberal—or cleft capitalist—system under Mubarak, which ultimately boosted the securitization of the polity that continues today. The purpose of this chapter is to look beyond youth as a social cohort, since the wider social, economic, and political spheres shape the meaning and agency of young people.[58]

Chapter 2 further develops the political economy of youth approach through analyzing the extent to which "youth" as a generational unit has been a central preoccupation of political regimes in Egypt since Nasser. The Nasser regime in particular was aware of youth's ability to instigate change as a consequence of the Free Officers' own heritage as members of several political youth groups.[59] It also analyzes the dynamics of youth policies under Sadat.[60] The chapter assesses the youth strategies of the Mubarak regime and subsequently the al-Sisi regime, while emphasizing the general discourse about youth during this period. Here the power relations within the polity are discussed, with their "diverse relations and settings, processes and organizations."[61] This analysis engages critically with the historical processes shaping the regime narrative toward youth, what the regime believes they should do, and how they should be regulated and governed.[62]

While the second part analyzes the agency of young people within this system, I ask the deeper question of how much the polity influences the young and how the young influence the polity. Chapters 3, 4, and 5 move from structure to agency. They analyze the impact of the securitized, neoliberal (cleft capitalist) system on the agency of young people. They discuss how young people shape, organize, and perceive the economic and political structures in Egypt.[63] Chapter 3 focuses on the dilemmas that young people face as a result of their civic and political engagement in the formal sphere. It analyzes how they are perceived as the hope of the nation, yet securitization and repression are also applied against them. It demonstrates how they accept the boundaries and red lines set by the regime and also how they are critical of the increased securitization and repression in the polity.

Chapter 4 analyzes the impact of the political context on young activists today. It looks at who they are, their perceptions and aspirations for reform and change, and how repression and securitization are impacting their activism. Discussions are drawn from those who are members of human rights organizations, protest movements, opposition political parties, and student unions, as well as from independent activists in our sample.

Chapter 5 discusses young people from low-income backgrounds, or the poor and marginalized, and the extent to which those who are primarily from subaltern groups are marginalized within the polity. This chapter discusses youth insecurities and precarities and why many choose to exit the political scene.

Chapter 6 takes a more regional approach and analyzes the impact of authoritarianism and neoliberalism on young people in the MENA region, specifically in Turkey, the Occupied Palestinian Territories, Lebanon, Morocco, and Tunisia.

1

The Political Economy of Authoritarianism in Egypt

In April 2018, the World Bank reported the following about Egypt: "The implementation of reforms along with the gradual restoration of confidence and stability are starting to yield positive results. The economy is gradually improving with the annual rates of GDP growth reaching 4.3 percent in 2015/2016, and grew at 5.2% in H1-FY18, compared to 3.7% a year earlier, mainly driven by investment, exports and consumption."[1]

A month later, on May 14, 2018, the *Al-Shorouk* newspaper noted that "the security personnel took control of the metro stations yesterday, the first day of the working week, after the governments' decision to increase the prices of the metro tickets. The security personnel intensified their presence at all entrances and exit doors, deployed police dogs in anticipation of any emergency or illegal actions by individuals."[2]

The unmistakable message from these descriptions was that economic reform in Egypt is tightly linked to securing the regime. The authoritarian, neoliberal order in which the country finds itself today cannot be implemented without an increased presence of security personnel in the public space. Consequently, the relations of power within the polity can progressively add to the exploitative character of the ruling elite and its associated economic elite, against the social and economic interests of other groups, in particular the poor and the middle classes.[3] In this system, governments do not take on debt to stimulate the economy; instead, they shift the burden to their citizens, and it is the poor who incur most debt.[4] The following analysis of the historical development of the political economy of authoritarianism adds to our understanding of the larger economic, social, and political contexts. The chapter looks at the historical development of the "macro material and ideological conditions" that have been developing in Egypt since Gamal Abdel Nasser's ascendance to power until today.[5]

Nasser and the Establishment of the "Deep State"

Nasser's legacy in Egypt is manifold. He secured his hold on power in 1954 after a brief power struggle between him and his followers against Mohamed Naguib, the then-president of the newly established republic.[6] Nasser succeeded in establishing an authoritarian regime that has been ruled by military strongmen for more than six decades, with only one year of civilian rule. Not only was he capable of building this authoritarian state, but he also constructed a national narrative that endorsed the military as a legitimate institution that forms a powerful praetorian guard over the nation. In such a regime, the bureaucracy, the regime's repressive apparatus, and the international community all play an important role in ensuring the regime's survival.[7] Nevertheless, the extension of economic control through the public sector or through the control of natural resources, and the co-optation of business elites, has an even greater impact on the longevity and survivability of authoritarian regimes.

The authoritarian system founded by Nasser has lasted these decades by changing the social base of the previous monarchical regime, purging all political opposition, and gaining legitimacy with the masses through agrarian reform measures and the Import Substitution and Industrialization (ISI) developmental model. The deep state that he then created was composed "primarily of the military, intelligence and presidential institutions, among which and from which extend both formal relationships and informal networks. The latter are utilitarian rather than effective, born out of self-interest or friendships, but not out of deeper social formations."[8]

Nasser relied heavily on the military, from which he would select personnel who enjoyed his confidence and appoint them to bureaucratic posts. In 1964, for instance, almost twenty-two of the twenty-six regional governors were army officers or former army officers.[9] More than three-quarters of bureaucrats in the Ministry of the Interior were also either army officers or retired officers.[10] The growth in the urban bureaucracy and of public-sector employment in urban managerial positions, especially for young, educated people, presented an opportunity for the rural elite to send their sons and daughters to urban areas to seek state employment. According to Hazem Kandil, the new bureaucratic class mainly consisted of the sons of rural elites: "Soon these young bureaucrats transformed the public sector into a labyrinth of commercial and financial fiefdoms, which supplemented the agricultural fiefdoms their families had established in the countryside. Strategically placed in the city and the countryside, this new elite now represented the bulwark of the ruling party, the [Arab Socialist Union, or] ASU."[11]

These dynamics developed a web of interests between the security apparatus—the army and the Ministry of the Interior—and the rising economic elite, who were already working in the public sector to sustain the authoritarian regime and advance their own interests. At the same time, Nasser clamped down on citizens' political participation in order to entrench his rule. He also took advantage of personal rivalries between military personnel to extend his domination over the polity. He permitted only a small number of the political elite into the policy-making circle, and these were exclusively army officers. Civilians who occupied ministerial offices or other important jobs were technocrats, with brief tenures in office. Nasser further ensured that he could dominate these powerful elites by fragmenting them. Hence, personal alliances were essential within the various institutional settings. For instance, one major group with considerable influence was present in the ASU, led by Ali Sabri, while another was centered around the security apparatus, headed by Sami Sharaf. Other power centers were in the executive branch, with Anwar Sadat in charge.[12] All of these were subordinate to Ali Sabri, a member of the Free Officers movement with left leanings. This developed into a clientelistic network, which forced Nasser to direct policy outcomes to the advantage of his clients rather than pursuing the developmental model he had favored.[13]

Sadat and Infitah

After Nasser's sudden death in 1970, Sadat became president and initiated major socioeconomic and political changes in 1971, in the form of a permanent constitution and a National Action Program.[14] In May 1971 he announced a "Corrective Revolution" to consolidate power, and he used it to purge Nasserists from the political and security establishments.[15] He publicly exposed an attempted coup d'état against him, led by Sabri, then head of the ASU and vice president of Egypt, which facilitated the latter's removal from office. Internationally this was an important strategy, since Sabri was mainly backed by the Soviet Union. Accordingly, Sadat started his first signs of shifting allegiance from the Soviet Union to the United States. He arrested ninety-one army officials, of whom six were ministers, in addition to a large number of ASU executives, parliamentarians, bureaucrats, and media officials. He also developed an emergency court to try the coup plotters, who received long prison sentences.[16] "The heads of the army, the police, the party, the intelligence apparatus and the information apparatus rolled with remarkable ease, once they had been charged with plotting against the regime."[17] Shortly afterward he reorganized the executive, mainly the ministerial cabinet, appointed new governors whom he personally trusted, expelled many members of the National Assembly, and reduced the power of the police and the intelligence and information apparatuses.

Only a few months into his presidency, Sadat was able to secure control over the polity.[18] He rapidly increased the power of the Ministry of the Interior and the State Security Investigations Service (SSIS), its chief spy organ, to counterbalance the power of the army.[19] He then developed policies to demilitarize his regime, to reduce the economic influence of officers, and to marginalize their influence in politics. Whenever an officer retired from civil service, he was replaced by a civilian. During Sadat's tenure in office, only 7.5 percent of ministers were from the officer corps, and only five out of twenty-six governors were military officers.[20]

The Market-Oriented Economy

Having secured political control, Sadat developed and announced a new economic program in the October Working Paper of 1974. Known as *infitah*, or opening the door to capital investment by domestic and foreign investors, this document summed up his economic outlook as "Arab capital + Western technology + abundant Egyptian manpower and other resources = development and progress."[21] New laws were promulgated to increase the role of the private sector in the market, to end state monopoly over trade, to ease restrictions on banks, to facilitate the flow of foreign direct investments, and to decrease restrictions on imports.[22] The World Bank and the International Monetary Fund (IMF) had first set out economic conditionalities for Egypt as early as 1962, under Nasser's rule. However, during Sadat's tenure and after the October War of 1973 in particular, these conditionalities became embedded in the Egyptian economy, leading to the securitization of the new market-oriented economy and to the neoliberal system in place today. In 1976, Egypt entered a standby agreement with both international institutions. Major features of the reform and structural adjustment processes were to reduce subsidies on some consumer goods, to lower the budget deficit, to regulate exchange-rate policies, and to ease foreign trade.[23] Some elements of these policies were aborted when the first attempt at reducing subsidies sparked bread riots in 1977.[24]

Nevertheless, the economic outlook for Egypt was considered to be positive by the international community. The peace treaty with Israel at the end of the October War of 1973 delivered an economic and military aid package for both Egypt and Israel from the United States. From it, Egypt received US$1.5 billion in military loans and US$300 million in economic aid. The military aid was in the form of loans through a Foreign Military Sales program, which stretched over three years.[25] The peace treaty stimulated tourism, generating US$700 million in revenues by 1980. In addition, the oil boom of the 1970s brought an unprecedented growth in labor migration to Libya and the Arab Gulf countries. This amounted to an increase in foreign currency through the remittances received. By 1980, Egyptian foreign workers' remittances amounted to US$3 billion per annum.[26] The majority of migrants' savings was sent back to Egypt, and a large number of migrants returned to Egypt to join its expanding business class. Construction companies sprang up and a real estate boom lasted throughout the 1970s. Foreign direct investments and local agencies for foreign companies increased from a few dozen in the early 1970s to 16,000 by 1981.[27] The role of the army in the economy was sharply reduced, as a result of the privatization of state-owned enterprises that had been managed by army officers.[28]

Between 1974 and 1985, Egypt's GDP per capita doubled from US$334 to US$700. However, the economy was volatile and vulnerable to international shocks due to its reliance on rents and the surge in corruption.[29] Even though many attempts at both privatization and encouraging foreign direct investments were made, the private sector remained small during the Sadat era. By the time Sadat's term ended with his assassination in October 1981, publicly owned enterprises comprised almost 60 percent of manufacturing output value, and the public sector amounted to 22 percent of the total value added to the Egyptian economy.[30] According to World Bank estimates, public spending between 1974 and 1981 increased from 48 percent of GDP to 62 percent.[31]

Political Liberalization

Securing the power of the regime became essential to develop the political liberalization process. Sadat thus allocated more powers to the Ministry of the Interior, the security services, and the police. The rise in number of jihadi groups and of supporters of political Islam in general justified such an increase.[32] In addition, Sadat's Corrective Revolution identified certain principles to be followed by the elite, especially by individuals who held high positions in the public sector, the media, and the state apparatus. These principles were mainly to protect social peace and national unity, to uphold religious and spiritual values and due process of law, and to protect workers' and peasants' achievements. The principles were deliberately vague, so that Sadat would have the upper hand against anyone who would challenge his edicts. He also created the Law of Shame, which became useful in cracking down on unwanted dissent. It applied to the dissemination of any religious or political criticism by individuals against the regime.[33] A few years later Sadat allowed free parliamentary elections and opened the way to a multiparty system in which right, left, and center would compete. In the meantime he established a centrist party, which later became the National Democratic Party (NDP) and the center of political organization until the ouster of Hosni Mubarak in 2011.[34]

The infitah policies increased and extended the patronage system established by Nasser, creating a new economic and political elite dependent on Sadat for their affluence and political power.[35] These elites were not only businessmen who developed the private sector, but also public-sector employees and bureaucrats who had become major benefactors of Sadat's policies. According to Nazih Ayubi, the public sector soon became mired in corruption, since its officials were paid low wages.[36] Thus, the institutionalization of corruption was rampant under Sadat.[37] For instance, a large number of bureaucrats would accept foreign direct investments in order to receive sizable commissions, even if these investments would not add to the country's economic progress or to the improvement of citizens' living standards. Even in the agricultural sector, many private investors bought agricultural land more cheaply than the general market prices. Sadat was aware of these corrupt practices and was determined to conceal them. He would punish any whistleblower who exposed corruption in the public realm, while personally ensuring that businessmen engaged in corruption would have impunity.[38]

For Sadat, personal loyalty was more important than political institutions and organizations.[39] Robert Springborg argues that "personal connections and access remain as crucial in Sadat's as they were in Nasser's Egypt[;] only the organizational framework within which they are established has changed."[40] In one obvious example, Sadat married his daughter to the son of the People's Assembly speaker, and easing media censorship was accompanied by placing trusted individuals in editorial positions in the major news outlets.[41] Even in the military, Sadat ensured personal rather than institutional allegiance. He frequently rotated and changed military appointments and leadership positions to ensure personal allegiance to himself. He played off intramilitary rivalries so that no power base could emerge from the military institution.[42]

Mubarak and Structural Adjustment

The assassination of Sadat by a member of Islamic Jihad in 1981 while he was celebrating the anniversary of the October War victory—in a secured area that was supposed to be protected by the military—dealt a savage blow to the status quo. When Hosni Mubarak became president, he incrementally and cautiously moved away from Sadat's policies to advance his own sociopolitical and economic views.

Mubarak assumed the presidency at a time when public spending was high as a ratio of GDP and when the regime had enormous revenues from the Suez Canal, from migrant workers' remittances, and from foreign aid, in addition to tax revenues. Nevertheless, a few years into his rule, revenues started to decrease due to the end of the oil boom, the surge in Egyptian population, and the reduction in development aid.[43] Mubarak's official discourse was against Sadat's infitah policy, and he encouraged the political opposition to criticize it. During the first decade of his rule he wanted to boost industrialization in both public and private sectors. He enacted some protective barriers to imports, lowered interest rates on investment loans, and reduced taxes on industrial profits to 32 percent compared to 40 percent on other commercial sectors.

The result was an expansion in the industrial and private sectors, especially in automobile assembly and manufacturing and in the clothing industries.[44] During this decade, Mubarak was hesitant to reduce subsidies and impose major economic restructuring, so that his policies were neither fully market-oriented nor socialist.[45]

Mubarakism in the 1980s

The economic outlook, however, was declining during the 1980s, with oil prices and Suez Canal revenues dropping to almost half of their peaks in the previous decade. Oil income fell from US$2.26 billion to US$1.2 billion and Canal revenue from US$1 billion to US$900 million in only one year. The United States also held back US$265 million of its financial aid to Egypt until the government committed to the economic reforms prescribed by the IMF.[46] Thus in 1987 Egypt signed an economic reform package with the IMF, obligating the country to introduce some reforms. Egypt was required to reduce public spending and liquidate public companies, while liberalizing the market for more private-sector investments. It was also required to devalue the Egyptian pound vis-à-vis the US dollar and to raise interest rates to encourage savings and reduce consumption.[47] In return, the Paris Club approved a rescheduling of Egypt's foreign debt. Mubarak did not, however, reduce spending, but actually increased it from 54 percent of GDP in 1986 to 57.2 percent in 1987. The budget deficit also rose by three percentage points in the same period, causing extreme volatility in the Egyptian economy.[48] When Egypt joined the international allied forces against Saddam Hussein's invasion of Kuwait, the international community, mainly the creditor countries, agreed to cancel half of its foreign debt, but Egypt was forced to implement the IMF and World Bank conditionalities for economic development.[49]

Mubarak, unlike Sadat, increased the role of the military in the economic sector in an attempt to coup-proof his rule. The Minister of Defense at that time, Abdel Halim Abu Ghazala, was able to secure military "aid" instead of a "loan" from the United States. From 1986 onward, the annual military aid to Egypt from the United States amounted to US$1.3 billion.[50] This enhanced the military's ability to secure services for the officers' corps, such as subsidized housing and food products in addition to clubs exclusively for officers. The National Service Products Organization (NSPO), set up after the peace treaty with Israel, was intended to assimilate the surplus of officers into economic development projects, but it soon became an economic powerhouse in its own right.[51] The NSPO, in addition to other military corporations, developed a range of industries and construction companies and acquired desert land for agricultural cultivation. It also promoted a new discourse about the valuable contribution of the military to the country's economic development. In these activities the military was in direct competition with the private sector. It justified its market penetration by claiming that the products it generated were necessary for the self-sufficiency of the armed forces. The military narrative by the 1990s was that its intervention in the market controlled soaring prices and enhanced the welfare of low-income families.[52]

The government bureaucracy became another sphere of influence for the military. Mubarak appointed retired military generals and colonels to many bureaucratic positions. Retired army officers once again became governors, and they ran administrations in important locations such as tourist centers in Sinai and Upper Egypt. Oil-sector enterprises also became militarized, with retired generals taking charge of many publicly owned natural gas and oil companies.[53]

While the long arm of military control was flexing in the economy and bureaucracy, the roles of the Ministry of the Interior, the security forces, and the police were also expanding. The rise of Islamic Jihad, especially after the attempted assassination of Mubarak in Ethiopia in 1995, was another justification for increasing the power of the security forces in the polity. Its annual budget rose from $1.058 billion in the 1990s to $3.78 billion in 2008.[54] By 2009, the Ministry of the Interior employed 1.7 million individuals, of whom 850,000 were police personnel and administrative staff, 450,000 were Central Security Forces, and 400,000 belonged to the State Investigation Services. The regime also funded a new type of security force dependent on regime-paid thugs, or *baltagya*. "Baltagya are criminals with a record of violence, who are paid to carry out duties of 'disciplining' members of the public in return for the police turning a blind eye to their criminal activities, including drug trafficking."[55]

The Development of the Neoliberal System of Sorts

The "Ten Commandments" of the Washington Consensus, which are the core of neoliberal economic policies, are as follows: low budget deficits; redirection of public expenditure from politically sensitive fields to neglected areas with higher economic returns; tax reforms; financial liberalization; a unified exchange rate; the reduction of trade restrictions; abolishing barriers to the entry of foreign direct investments; privatization of public enterprises; facilitation of regulations to increase the entry of new firms into the market; and reforming the legal system to secure property rights.[56] The most significant impact of neoliberalism on the lives of citizens, especially the poor, is on social security, through the privatization and commercialization of social programs.[57]

The Egyptian economy is a "national variety of globalized neoliberalism."[58] Economic growth was confined to a small number of capital-intensive sectors, whose capacity to generate employment opportunities was low.[59] Neoliberalism should be regarded as an international political project based on a class strategy that enhances "accumulation by dispossession."[60] It does not, in Egypt's case, signify the rollback of the state. On the contrary, it means the rolling back of certain state functions, particularly in development areas, such as the state's role in healthcare, education, and employment.[61]

To maintain this economic system, Egypt, like other Arab regimes, perpetuated exclusionary and repressive policies.[62] State institutions took over the privatization process, either through passing new legislation or by developing new committees "dedicated to fast-tracking the decisions around privatization. . . . In all cases, the development and execution of economic policy has been distanced as far as possible from any control or influence of legislative bodies within the state."[63] In addition, a crony capitalist system was established, in which political decision-makers were unwilling to include the quickly eroding middle class or the high number of socially and economically excluded youth. In 2005, Transparency International ranked Egypt at 70 out of 158 countries, but by 2008 Egypt had fallen to 115 out of 180 countries.[64]

From the late 1990s, the Mubarak regime embarked on more forceful economic liberalization. New measures were introduced: an acceleration of privatization, cuts in social expenditure, legal reforms to introduce flexibility in employment, and the removal of trade barriers.[65] For instance, subsidies to the transport sector were reduced, while public investments were held at 11 percent of GDP by the early 2000s.[66] Tariffs were also slashed from an average of 42.2 percent in 1991 to 19.9 percent by 2005. Industrial exports, on the other hand, stagnated at 37 percent from the early 1990s until 2007. During the Mubarak years, especially the first decade of the 2000s, businessmen, bureaucrats, and trade unionists became the second circle of elites after Mubarak.[67] These groups were able to infiltrate the political sphere and influence Mubarak about the "reform" of legislation on working hours and unionism. They also established strong ties with the media and press, to ensure their visibility and to influence the public discourse on the importance of a free-market economy and the neoliberal system. In 2004 when a new prime minister, Ahmed Nazif, was appointed, his cabinet was called the "businessmen's cabinet."[68] It represented the embedding of a new political class, which was networked with Mubarak and his family through economic interests that marked the apogee of crony capitalism. By the end of 2010, the international financial institutions that endorsed neoliberalism viewed Egypt's economic development as positive. "Mubarak's Egypt was a poster child for a new neoliberal order in the region. For several years it had been hailed by the World Bank for its 'reforms' as one of the world's top-ten most improved economies."[69]

In 2010, the Economist Intelligence Unit named Egypt as among the next round of emerging markets.[70] In spite of these positive economic assessments, the forcibly imposed neoliberal policies have had a severe negative impact on citizens' daily subsistence levels. When the spark of the Arab uprisings was lit in Tunisia, it quickly spread to Egypt, leading to Mubarak's ouster.[71] With hindsight, international financial institutions have acknowledged the structural problems caused by neoliberalism in Egypt, and that the private sector created an environment in which the informal sector increased, with its associated low wages and poor working conditions. They also realized that profitable private-sector firms did not generate sufficient jobs, and even when jobs were prevalent, secure contracts and provision for social security were rare in the Egyptian context.[72]

Political Liberalization and Repression

Political liberalization was an important pillar of the Mubarak regime. Unlike his predecessors, Mubarak attempted to compensate for the drastic economic liberalization measures by liberalizing the public sphere. A relatively free media and press was tolerated even when it criticized the regime's political and economic policies.[73] For example, the media extensively attacked corruption in both public and private sectors. The regime tolerated these criticisms as long as they did not target Mubarak, who remained a red line until shortly before the January 25, 2011 uprising. Yet the regime did nothing to stop corruption.[74] Political parties and charity organizations were also tolerated, in part because the activities of civil society organizations were important in sustaining the neoliberal process, especially with the decrease of government spending on social welfare. However, strong restrictions on civil society work were the rule rather than the exception, even though the number and scope of nongovernmental organizations (NGOs) increased from 7,593 in 1985 to 24,449 in 2008.[75] Half of these organizations are developmental and religious, while the rest relate to sports, youth, social clubs, and trade and industry chambers, in addition to professional syndicates, trade unions, and workers' unions.

The Mubarak regime maintained a tight grip on civil society organizations through legal measures, at first through Law 32 from 1964, enacted under Nasser to restrict civil society. In 2002 that law was updated to accommodate the neoliberal trend, becoming Law 84 of 2002.[76] This law banned civil society organizations from engaging in political activities or in any activity that is threatening "national unity, violating public order or morals, or calling for discrimination between citizens of race, origin, color, language, religion or creed."[77] The Mubarak regime was most tolerant of business associations and development organizations, which in turn relied on the regime for the protection and enhancement of their economic interests.[78]

Political participation and parliamentary elections were encouraged. In 1987, for instance, parliamentary elections resulted in an unprecedented 30 percent of members of parliament belonging to the opposition. In response, the Supreme Constitutional Court dissolved the parliament on the basis of the unconstitutionality of combining both proportional representation and single-member districts. A new law was promulgated, permitting only single-member district representation. Two members were to be elected for each district in a winner-takes-all electoral system. In response, the opposition boycotted the 1990 parliamentary elections on the ground that it would not be fairly represented in parliament. However, many members of the opposition parties ran as independents, which added to the rifts and internal feuds in the already-weak parties. The result, inevitably, was the dominance of the NDP in parliamentary representation.[79]

An important strategy of Mubarak and his NDP associates during the 1990s and early 2000s was to gather most independent candidates into the ranks of the NDP. This tactic upheld the interests of the independents, while ensuring that laws concerning the general governance of the country would be in favor of Mubarak and his supporters. Independent candidates who belonged to the Muslim Brotherhood, however, were largely tolerated by the regime and were allowed to contest parliamentary seats either as independents or as candidates with other secular political parties.[80]

During this time, repression of political contenders, labor movements, and the urban poor was high. For instance, when in 2003 demonstrations were held against the American-led invasion of Iraq, almost 1,500 people were arrested and beaten while in custody.[81] More importantly, when Saad Eddin Ibrahim, an American University in Cairo sociology professor, called on the United States to link economic aid to Egypt's human rights' performance, he was sentenced to two years in prison for "tainting Egypt's image abroad."[82] Torture and police brutality against political opposition also increased during this period. The torturing to death of a young man, Khaled Said, mobilized large numbers of activists against regime repression. The regime responded to workers' strikes and other protest activities during the early 2000s with both carrot and stick. It sometimes yielded to their demands, for example by offering better salaries, but at other times protest leaders were imprisoned and tortured by state security personnel.[83]

Security personnel also used excessive violence and repression against the poor, especially the urban subaltern groups, whose numbers and presence both in the informal economy and in informal settlements have surged since the mid-1990s.[84] The use of violence against citizens through forced evictions from informal settlements has been extensive.[85] Collective punishment campaigns against subaltern groups also intensified. For instance, in 2005 the police stormed into a village and attacked its farmers, who refused to be evicted from the land they cultivated in the Delta village of Sarando.[86]

January 2011 and the Rise of the al-Sisi Regime

When Mubarak was ousted in 2011, the Supreme Council of the Armed Forces (SCAF) took charge in the interim. Since 2011, Egypt has had a series of rulers—SCAF, Mohamed Morsi, Adly Mansour, and Abdel

Fattah al-Sisi—but the common denominator has been the growing power of the military in the polity. Military leaders have also been collaborating closely with the Ministry of the Interior. This collaboration is at the heart of the political economy of authoritarian survival today.[87]

In the 2012–2013 fiscal year the budget deficit rose to almost 12 percent of GDP, while social expenditure increased and government revenues decreased. External rents from oil, natural gas, and the Suez Canal, and grants from aid agencies have either declined or stagnated since 2011, while government expenditure has remained high at almost 30 percent of GDP. This is due to the high spending on certain regime interests, in particular public-sector wages, universal subsidies, and oil subsidies. Oil subsidies amounted to almost 20 percent of total government expenditure in 2008.[88] On the other hand, according to World Bank estimates, Egypt's GDP growth fell from 7.15 percent in 2008 to 2.21 percent in 2012, while unemployment increased from 8.7 percent in 2008 to 12.7 percent in 2012, its highest point since 1991.[89]

The military ouster of Morsi in 2013 brought in a military-backed interim government headed by Adly Mansour, chief judge of the Supreme Constitutional Court.[90] Under Mansour the economy remained constrained, with the same problems precipitating unemployment, budgetary constraints, and lack of tourism revenues. There were no reformist economic policies during this period, but state-led violence increased, with a surge in arbitrary arrests and detentions according to Amnesty International.[91]

The NDP was dissolved in 2011 by a court order, and so far no dominant political party has emerged. The official discourse in the media argues that al-Sisi does not "need" a dominant political party, since he is highly popular.[92] Nevertheless, in the 2020 parliamentary elections, the Mostaqbal Watan Party (Nation's Future Party) won 316 out of 596 seats, compared to 53 seats in the 2015 parliament. It is widely believed that the party's close relations with the security apparatus is the main reason for its rise to prominence.[93] Civil society organizations have been increasingly restricted and repressed since 2011. The latest attempt to diminish their role in the public sphere was made through a new NGO law in 2017, which was ratified by al-Sisi in spite of international and national opposition. This law stated that NGOs are allowed to engage only in developmental activities that "conform to national development plans."[94] Failure to do so will lead to imprisonment. "NGOs may not conduct work that harms 'national security,' 'law and order,' 'public morals,' or 'public health,' terms that are subject to discretionary interpretation of government agencies."[95] A new organization, the National Authority for the Regulation of Non-governmental Foreign Organizations, is to be established to oversee civil society, in place of previous oversight from the Ministry of Social Solidarity. This organization is to be composed of representatives from the Ministry of Defense, Ministry of the Interior, Foreign Ministry, Ministry of Justice, the General Intelligence Directorate, the Administrative Control Authority, the Ministry of International Cooperation, and the Money Laundering Unit.[96]

The new constitution ratified in 2014 gave extra-judicial powers to the military with no judicial oversight. The military controlled, and still controls, a "hidden economy" within the Egyptian economy. Estimates of the role of the military in the economy vary from 20 to 40 percent. "The broad margin given to this estimate reflects the dearth of knowledge and lack of transparency surrounding the issue. As it stands now, military firms enjoy favourable tax treatment and are subsidized through the financial assistance they receive from the government defence budget."[97] The NSPO, in addition to other military-affiliated companies, has expanded at an unprecedented rate. Its economic activities have also pushed into new economic sectors like fish farming, pharmaceutical manufacturing, development of housing sites, and educational institutions.[98] Robert Springborg estimates that the military directly and indirectly accounts for almost 8 percent of all jobs in Egypt today.[99]

The same neoliberal model established under Mubarak's rule still prevails under al-Sisi. Economic policy changes have mainly targeted big businesses and foreign direct investments from the Gulf. Al-Sisi slashed subsidies but kept social policies unchanged to mitigate the economic hardship suffered by the majority of the population. The first wave of economic reforms under his tenure focused on rebalancing the macro-economic aspects of the economy.[100] These included a new Value-Added Tax (VAT) law, lower energy subsidies, and the flotation of the Egyptian pound.[101] The relationship between businessmen and the regime has radically changed under successive presidents, and in particular since al-Sisi's ascendance in 2014. Tycoon businessmen were seen in 2014 as a liability, since their corrupt dealings with the Mubarak regime had been publicly exposed during the 2011 uprising.[102]

Under al-Sisi the locally adopted neoliberal structure has become more controlled and militarized through different yet similar means of repression. Repression has been extensively utilized against all forms of dissent, especially against the Muslim Brotherhood and its adherents and during parliamentary elections. Nevertheless, the view of international financial institutions on Egypt's economic growth is upbeat, with the World Bank asserting that the implementation of economic reforms and the gradual political stability are yielding positive effects, which have led to 5.2 percent growth in GDP in 2018, compared to only 2 percent in 2014.[103]

Conclusion

The early development of the political economy of authoritarianism has led to the authoritarian, securitized, neoliberal system in Egypt today. The political economy of authoritarian survival embraced by Egypt's rulers is based on patronage, cronyism, and co-opting the economic and political elites. Nasser's development of a deep state in Egypt was essential for embedding and perpetuating the securitized, neoliberal regime. All presidents since Nasser have deftly exploited the economic and political systems to their advantage, by depending either on favored security personnel from the army in the case of Nasser and al-Sisi; on the army and Ministry of the Interior in the case of Mubarak; or on the Ministry of the Interior in the case of Sadat. This political economy of authoritarianism requires a national narrative to justify it and simultaneously to accommodate the growing number of young people living within this structure.

2

The Construction of Youth in Egyptian Politics

The relationship between the regime and young people in Egypt is highly complex. To understand this relationship and how it develops the meaning and positioning of young people in a different time and space, this chapter examines the context of political struggle over youth politics. Here I look at how the regime "frame[s] and shape[s] the lives of young people."[1] Some strategies, especially strategies of depoliticization, have changed over the decades while others like repression have remained constant. From the regime's perspective, young people should comply with its main ideologies and accept their own positioning within the polity. The subsequent regimes from Nasser until today have used youth to deepen their dominant political and economic power; hence young people are used as a "social construct for political-economic ends."[2] In this sense these regimes have constructed a narrative of youth as a hope/promise and as a threat/peril to the nation. Young people who accept the authoritarian structure, want to work within it, and can be politically co-opted are regarded as the hope. The regime can contain this group through policies that regulate political participation and by fostering their economic, cultural, and social participation. On the other hand, "revolutionary" young people, or those who resort to street politics to reform the authoritarian system from below, are portrayed as a threat or peril to the nation.

Nasser's Dilemma of Youth as Promise or Peril?

The 1952 coup d'état prepared the ground for a new political regime that had young people at its core. The Free Officers who staged the coup were all aged in their early to mid-thirties.[3] Initially, they chose Major

General Mohamed Naguib as their figurehead, in the belief that his seniority would grant them more credibility.[4] After a two-year power struggle, Gamal Abdel Nasser and the younger officers were able to curb the old guard backing Naguib and later to dispense with Naguib himself. From then until Nasser's death, the political scene was dominated by Nasser and his followers.[5]

This struggle between the old and the new guards in the military exposed the paradox of youth as the hope for the nation's future and youth as a threat. On the one hand, Nasser and the Revolutionary Command Council (RCC) were "young" and "revolutionary" since they had toppled the long-standing Egyptian monarchy and even got rid of the older leadership in the army, yet on the other hand, they needed to secure their grip on political power. The Nasserists believed in the importance of young people in the political process, and they developed various political institutions to incorporate youth into their ranks, while building a large bureaucracy whose backbone was young university graduates.

Nasser developed different strategies toward young people. He attempted to gain legitimacy through ensuring employment opportunities for all university graduates in the state bureaucracy. He encouraged young people's politicization in only two spheres: anticolonial struggle, and participation in the dominant political party, the Arab Socialist Union (ASU).[6] Street politics or demonstrations were intolerable. In his early attempts to gain control over the polity, Nasser's speeches to young people demonstrated his belief in the importance of young people as a force for development and decolonization. In one of his speeches to young university students, for instance, he argued, "The nation needs every one of you, we need you all to work with us, we are all Egyptians and have one goal. . . . I have heard a lot about freedom of expression. . . . [F]reedom of expression is provided for all; however, there are limits to freedom. Freedom is guaranteed for citizens; however, we cannot provide freedom to traitors."[7] This was one of the early attempts to set the stage for a broader discourse concerning the importance of those who are with us (i.e., the promise) versus those who are against us (i.e., the peril).

Nasser's social policies benefited young people through the material and social benefits they provided, and in return he received their extensive support. The regime funded free education for all and guaranteed employment for university graduates. The ongoing political socialization of young people was based on rejecting the key concepts of political parties, pluralism, democracy, and political participation. It inculcated the importance of the "revolution" as a means of defaming the previous monarchical regime and promoting Arab nationalism.[8]

Early Stages of Contestation against the Regime

At the height of the political struggle between the old and the new guards in the officer corps in 1954, a major debate developed on how to proceed with the post-coup political outlook. Naguib and his followers favored a parliamentary system based on political parties, while Nasser and his supporters wanted stability and state-led development.[9] Nasser was opposed to liberal constitutionalism, to the multiparty system, and to political parties in general, and he often portrayed these as having failed to decolonize the country and as being instruments of the monarchy and the landed elites against the poor.[10] The resistance of the 1952 to 1954 period was primarily led by university students, who formed a coalition or "national union," which turned university campuses into centers of demonstrations against the regime for almost a month.[11]

Cairo University, for instance, was a battleground between RCC forces and student activists. The students set up a student front from which they mobilized against military rule and called for democracy in Egypt.[12] As a consequence, classes were not allowed to resume, and by mid-April 1953 only the fourth-year classes (i.e., the seniors) were permitted to return to their studies. Many student activists and university professors who voiced criticism against the RCC were imprisoned.[13]

During the summer break of the same year, the regime took legal action against the universities: it replaced most of the administrative boards of Egypt's three main public universities—Cairo, Ain Shams, and Alexandria; forty professors who participated in the demonstrations against the regime earlier in the year were dismissed; and, most importantly, the universities were brought under the direct control of the Ministry of Higher Education. Since then, university presidents, deans, and vice deans have been appointed by the ministry rather than by the faculty.[14] New regulations banned university students from all political activities, except in government-related organizations. The regime also banned student union elections, and from 1953 until 1959 it appointed to the unions only those students of whom it approved.[15] The regime's repression against activism was a clear message to young people at the time, especially those who were interested in political participation: either they participated through the formal sphere that is tolerable for the regime, or they would be repressed. Even if some activists would still be willing to continue their activism and take the risk, the space in Egypt's major universities for real political voice and social participation beyond the regime's control was closed off.

Co-optation and Depoliticization Strategies

In an effort to contain and control the "revolutionary" tendencies of the youth who were perceived as a threat against the regime, Nasser founded the ASU party in 1961. It was portrayed as a comprehensive alliance of all Egyptians from different backgrounds, including peasants, workers, students, intellectuals, and even capitalists.[16] A few years after its establishment, a youth wing, the Socialist Youth organization, was created.[17] This organization and its youthful members were presented as the hope of the nation. It was an essential tool for legitimating the regime and co-opting many young people into its ranks.

Nasser told the Socialist Youth that

youth is the backbone of the socialist union. . . . I believe we have young people that are [politically] aware. The youth's thinking and ideologies might not be very clear; however, through organization and clarification we can develop a strong force that protects our society. . . . [Y]outh that belong to the youth organization will be provided with privileges. In the military colleges we will give preferential treatment and privileges to members of [our] youth organizations. . . . [W]e will also provide privileges to members of the socialist youth organization. They will be more eligible for employment opportunities and they will have preferential treatment.[18]

Thus, those who chose to be co-opted in the system were given high positions in the bureaucracy, the military, and the government.[19] Nasser's charisma, in addition to his Arab nationalist sentiments, created a strong base for him among young people, especially those who wanted to be part of these organizations.[20] To further contain and mobilize them in support of his regime and its ideology, Nasser established a secret Arab Vanguard organization in 1965. Its purpose was to attract young people who would socialize and encourage other young people to work within the confines of the authoritarian system.[21] Accordingly, young people who were ambitious to become part of the social and political elite found the spaces to do so.

On the other hand, for the young people who were not part of these youth organizations, the regime developed a well-structured depoliticization process. This was mainly carried out on university campuses through organizations and clubs that were geared toward youth welfare and sports and not to politics.[22] A new national soccer team was another enticement to shift the attention of young people away from politics and toward sport.[23] Those young people who were interested in public service or had political ambitions in the aftermath of the 1952 coup had to accept the authority and political ideology of the Free Officers.

In spite of these compelling domestic policies, Egypt's defeat in the 1967 war against Israel was a major cause of youth contention against the regime. On February 21, 1968, students in Cairo University celebrated their Day of the Egyptian Student and engaged in some political discussions with government officials. They questioned the responsibility of high-ranking officials in the defeat and asked that they be put on trial. The government officials denied any wrongdoing. This led to demonstrations, which, for the first time since Nasser took power, went beyond the university gates. Young people organized demonstrations for six days on the streets of Cairo and Alexandria, which resulted in many arrests and detentions.[24] According to a then-student activist, young activists at the time believed that students had an enormous influence in mobilizing people for street contention: "students or youth in general have always been the spark behind every single action/movement in our modern history."[25] He argued that Nasser's declaration to resign from office was directly related to students' power on the street. Nevertheless, as a young person at the time, the activist faced two dilemmas: on the one hand he wanted to reform the system and democratize it, yet, on the other, he did not want to revert back to the monarchical system.

By the end of the year another youth mobilization, "the November 1968 intifada," erupted. By this time Nasser and his media machine had compiled a forceful rhetoric against the student movement, portraying it as a threatening rebellion against the state. It was claimed that the youth had been infiltrated by Western governments who sought to destabilize the nation during times of crisis.[26] The student union was brought under direct government supervision, and any individuals perceived as a threat were imprisoned without due process of law. Although the student movement was crushed at that time, it is now seen as the first sign of the youth movements that were to demonstrate against Sadat in the 1970s.[27]

The Sadat Regime and Youth

When Sadat became president in 1970 after Nasser's sudden death, he was faced with a legacy of socialist policies that favored public institutions and guaranteed youth employment. This was unsustainable in Sadat's vision of economic liberalization. Knowing, however, that economic liberalization would be unpopular among the majority of citizens, Sadat attempted to open up the political sphere and co-opt his opposition. His 1971 constitution allowed new political parties and permitted some political freedoms on university campuses.[28] He established three main factions to evolve out of the ASU—the center, the left, and the right—and by 1977 these had become separate political parties.[29] They constituted the "loyal" opposition. At this time Sadat emphasized the role of students in the future leadership of the country. He cancelled university guards and security personnel and also permitted the involvement of professors in student activities that were political, civic, and educational.[30]

Meanwhile, new youth movements had been in the making since the 1967 war, in four main trends: Islamists, Socialist Nasserists, Marxists, and Liberals.[31] Those who belonged to the "loyal" opposition, such as the Liberals and the Islamists, along with young people who were interested in charity work, were treated as the hope, while the others—mainly Marxists and Socialist Nasserists—were perceived to be the threat. The opening up of the political scene increased the politicization of young people, especially university students. This had begun with demonstrations inside university gates, but it led to mobilizing other citizens to demonstrate and culminated in occupying Tahrir Square for a day. The demonstrations called on Sadat to wage war against Israel to win back the Sinai Peninsula, which had been occupied by Israel after the 1967 war.[32] Ironically, the sit-in at Tahrir Square was on January 25, 1972, thirty-nine years prior to the 2011 uprising against Mubarak.[33]

After this incident, Sadat offered Islamist youth new opportunities to come to the fore in political life and especially on university campuses. He believed that this group would be the most capable of countering the Nasserists and Marxists, while at the same time it was being co-opted by the state.[34] The Islamist student movements gained public support and by 1974 student unions were taken over by Islamists, forcing leftist students to retreat on campus and in public life in general for the first time since the 1950s. These leftist students would soon graduate and dominate the various professional syndicates, especially those of the journalists, doctors, lawyers, and engineers.[35]

The regime used excessive repression against young people who posed a threat, especially the Nasserists and the Communist activists, since they had the highest mobilizational capabilities, even though their movements were still nascent.[36] As Adel Abdel Ghafar comments, "The regime also began to purposely conflate Marxism with Nasserism in its public discourse as it knew that Marxism had negative public connotations due to the perception that it was an atheist ideology."[37] A few years later, in 1977, young people were involved in other contentious events, especially the bread riots and demonstrations against Sadat's intended trip to Jerusalem. The bread riots caused a crisis for the regime, because they directly opposed Sadat's new economic liberalization policies, which entailed cutting subsidies on bread and other products. A broad base of mobilized citizens had been the backbone of the Nasser regime's legitimacy, and Sadat had to take action. He publicly denounced Nasserists and Communists for these contentious events. He argued that they exploited the nation and intended to seize political control. The bread riots were purposely called the "*intifada* of thieves."[38] This confrontation ended in a crackdown on most of the leftist and Nasserist intelligentsia, who were imprisoned without due process of law. To further contain and co-opt young people, the Sadat regime established the Council of Youth and Sports in 1979. It sponsored youth organizations and charity youth groups in universities, bringing many of the young people under the government's umbrella and regulating their activities through government supervision. The council was not, however, an important factor in the regime's policies until Sadat's death and Mubarak's rise to power.

Sadat's policies like those of his predecessor provided young people with the same message: either participate within the established red lines, or be repressed. A consequence of which is that many activists resorted to "exit" the political sphere, until another political opportunity erupted.

The Mubarak Regime and Youth

When Mubarak became president in 1981, he turned the Council of Youth and Sports into a ministry. In the 1980s and 1990s youth contention and student activism were low, and contained behind university doors. During the first two decades of his rule, Mubarak was mainly concerned with population-control policies. This was most evident when Egypt hosted the International Conference on Population and Development in September 1994. This event showed the regime's commitment to a development strategy in line with international institutions, especially the United Nations Development Programme (UNDP). The international community and international organizations spearheaded the framing of young people as partners in the global developmental process, in an attempt to entrench a global neoliberal system.[39] Within this context, then–First Lady Suzanne Mubarak became a public figure whose main role was to promote government–civil society partnerships. This was important in co-opting youth who were interested in charity and development work, and who also harbored political and social ambitions.

The Depoliticization of Youth

The 1990s witnessed another important phenomenon in line with international trends and new international donor conditionalities: a rise in the number and scope of nongovernmental organizations (NGOs). This therefore also increased the NGO-ization of the public sphere, as well as adding to the depoliticization of a large number of young people.[40]

By the end of the 1990s, the youth bulge was at its height, and the regime decided on some policy changes along with providing more opportunities for development-related NGOs to work with youth. The ruling National Democratic Party (NDP) defined youth as young people aged between eighteen and thirty-five. Studies of Egyptian youth portray them as older than this and argue that because of the increasing unemployment and the custom of late marriage, the upper age for youth should be increased to forty years.[41] In 2003, the regime enacted a national youth policy for the first time. It concentrated on global developmental issues, as had been set out by the UNDP's Millennium Development Goals (MDGs). Its major policies were directed at employment, political participation, health, population control, media, sports, environment, and social activities. The Mubarak regime viewed these developments, the growth in NGOs, and young people participating in these NGOs positively. These are examples of the promise/hope group. Officially, the NDP stated that youth policies should be aimed at the total youth population. In practice, the policies targeted in particular unemployed youth, young women, youth with special needs, and rural youth. However, this national plan was not legislated by the parliament or implemented by the government.[42] By this time a large number of young people were disinterested in politics. They had become depoliticized by successive political regimes and by Mubarak's own depoliticization strategies.

Nevertheless, similar to other contentious events during the past four decades, regional and internal dynamics triggered demonstrations against the regime. The new wave of contention started in 2001 in support of the al-Aqsa intifada and increased after the American-led invasion of Iraq in 2003. It began inside university campuses. However, young people mobilized others outside the campuses and in the major city squares.[43] Similar to 1977, young people occupied Tahrir Square in March 2003, as a sign of discontent with the Mubarak regime's failure to criticize the American-led invasion of Iraq.[44]

The Start of a New Wave of Youth Contention

This first wave of contention against the regime was followed by the founding of the Kifaya movement at the end of 2004. It attracted many young people, who later established their own youth movements, the first of which was the Youth for Change Movement. Young people once again moved their protests out of the universities and onto the streets. Blogging became an important medium for youth to criticize the regime. The Wael Abbas blog, for instance, was a space in which the independent activist Wael Abbas described torture in Egyptian police stations and uploaded images of torture incidents.[45] Other blogs followed suit, like the Misr Digital Blogspot, paving the way for more youth activism and contestation against the Mubarak regime. This was soon to increase with the establishment of the April 6 Youth Movement, created in solidarity with the al-Mahala workers' strike. It amalgamated the workers' socioeconomic grievances with those of young people, as well as with political grievances.[46] Like his predecessors, Mubarak utilized various strategies to co-opt the "liberal" containable youth, while repressing and imprisoning the "radical" youth who posed a threat to the regime.[47]

To counter this youth threat, the regime developed two strategies. The first was in the policy area, demonstrating the government's commitment to enhancing young people's living standards. Mubarak also revamped the Ministry of Youth and Sports and raised its visibility. He returned it into a Youth and Sports Council and in 2005 brought in a new director, Safey Eddin Kharboush, a professor of economics and political science at Cairo University. In the meantime, various government officials expressed their commitment to youth-sensitive policies. The Minister of Economic Development, Osman Mohamed Osman, announced that

the government is committed to develop and adopt a multidimensional concept of youth welfare that gives greater focus to the interrelated dimensions of education, access to ICT [information and communications technologies], employment and the quality of jobs, income levels, gender parity, health, civic participation, and so forth, and to translate these into an integrated strategy and action plan. The government is also committed to attain an equitable distribution of capabilities and opportunities for all of Egypt's youth.[48]

The establishment of sports and social centers was another means by which the regime sought to upgrade its youth policies. These centers, however, catered only to urban youth, in major cities, and access to the centers was restricted to young people who were regarded as loyal to whichever regime was in power. In our fieldwork with young people, a young man who works at a human rights organization argued that these centers cater only to youth who are either depoliticized or are loyal to the regime. "Young people from the political opposition or poor young people are denied access to these centers."[49] The few other youth centers located in rural areas soon became defunct.[50] According to a 2014 survey of young people in Egypt, only 1 percent of youth across the country were reported to be members of these youth clubs.[51] This reveals the sharp mismatch between what the government provided for youth and what the youth demands actually were. When addressing "the youth," the regime in general addressed the life experiences of middle-class rather than poor youth. Although its official discourse appeared positive regarding youth socioeconomic development, the policies enacted did not translate into a real commitment to medium-term and long-term strategies that created real development for all young people, regardless of class. The consequence of the politically endorsed, neoliberal economic system was that state policies and welfare were directed not at youth socioeconomic development, but to the benefit of Egypt's influential social and economic elites.

The second political strategy was political co-optation. The Mubarak regime actively co-opted young people through the benefits and perks it distributed through different ministries and councils, so that potential critics of the dictatorship who accepted these now had a vested interest in supporting the regime.[52] This involves a political exchange whereby the authoritarian leader exchanges rewards with his supporters, in a transaction that frequently turns into patronage.[53] The Mubarak regime introduced some political reforms in the early 2000s. A Party Congress in 2002 set up new committees, among which the Policies Committee, the Youth Committee, and the Training and Political Education Committee were important for advancing the political socialization of youth who were not considered threats. The NDP showed an interest in the development of youth cadres and encouraged young people to take leading positions in party ranks. By 2007, NDP elections ensured that within each committee at least one seat would be allocated to young people, and by 2009 that had increased to two seats. On several occasions, Mubarak remarked on the importance of bringing young people into party ranks and public policy circles because they could set the new vision and hope for Egypt's future.[54] The Future Generation Foundation (a government-sponsored initiative) had been established by Gamal Mubarak, the president's son, with most of its branches in public universities. It was developed as a vehicle through which young people could be incorporated into policy-making circles, and Gamal Mubarak managed it in an attempt to present himself as the champion of youth grievances.[55]

In 2005, the national student union election was predominantly won by young adherents to the then-ruling NDP. Some youth believed that this was due to heavy-handed government intervention in the electoral process. For instance, one focus-group participant was running for the student union presidency at a public university. This participant was told by the security personnel to become a member of the ruling NDP, as a condition for his election. When he refused to become a member of the NDP, his candidacy was dismissed.[56] As a consequence, a youth-led initiative called the Free Student Union was founded in 2005. This was a parallel student union in which students chose their own representatives, away from Ministry of the Interior constraints on who was allowed to run for the union leadership. Participation in these so-called free and independent elections was high, compared to the official student union elections.[57]

In another attempt at co-opting young people and countering the mounting pressure of the so-called radical youth (the threat) who were using cyberspace as a platform against the regime, the NDP established a Facebook forum to which it invited young people to discuss youth-related issues live with Gamal Mubarak. Another internet forum called Sharek (translated as "participate") encouraged political engagement and the political participation of young people through voting.[58] At al-Azhar University, the mouthpiece of the Ministry of Religious Affairs (Ministry of Awqaf), security interventions were high to bar the Muslim Brotherhood adherents from running or winning elections.

The Mubarak regime used the Ministry of Higher Education as an agent for co-optation and repression at the same time. The ministry's mission statement is that it should protect students' rights inside university campuses, and that it should be the sole guarantor of the right to education and of freedoms on campus. According to its various announcements, the ministry strove to develop the social, political, and sports activities of youth and to strengthen their capacity building. It also had the authority to oversee student unions and different activity groups like youth clubs.[59] In spite of its official mandate, on more than one occasion the Ministry of Higher Education failed to resist the encroachment of the Ministry of the Interior on university campuses. The Ministry of the Interior, with the acquiescence of the Ministry of Higher Education, enacted heavy-handed security and had an iron grip on university activities since Nasser's crackdown on universities in 1954. With one minor exception during the first years of Sadat's rule, there had been a heavy police presence inside universities, and freedom of speech exercised by both students and professors remained highly constrained.[60] Some attempts were made by the March 20 movement for Egyptian universities to be freed from a constant police presence, and in 2010 a court ruled that universities should no longer have a police force. However, in February 2014 the Court for Urgent Matters ruled that the police could return permanently to the universities.

The January 25 Uprising

The extent to which the Egyptian regime was committed to addressing youth issues was evident in the government's support for the UNDP's Egypt Human Development Report 2010, which was about youth in Egypt. The minister of economic development wrote its preface as a sign of interest in youth development and participation. However, this was not successful in fending off mobilization against the Mubarak regime. When large-scale demonstrations erupted in Tunisia at the end of 2010 Egyptian youth in late January 2011 were soon to mobilize in demonstrations against Mubarak, which would eventually oust him from power. As Maha Abdelrahman states:

> In fact, preparations and planning for the 25 January "day of rage" were coordinated by youth groups from different ideological backgrounds, including the 6 April Movement, Youth for Justice and Freedom, the Youth of El Gabha Party, the El-Baradei campaign and the MB [Muslim Brotherhood] Youth as well as the Facebook-based "We are all Khaled Said" group. . . . Quickly, and in response to the unexpected developments of the uprising and the perceived need to establish a body providing some form of representation, the Youth of the Revolution Coalition was formed on 6 February with two members from each of the above six groups.[61]

The regime used repressive measures, such as extra-judicial killings and imprisonments, and also resorted to counterdemonstrations, like the Battle of the Camels, in which regime supporters and thugs were sent to Tahrir Square to deal with the mobilized public on the streets.[62] The brutality of the police and the thugs against peaceful demonstrators was met with citizens' determination to maintain their sit-in at Tahrir Square, chanting, "We won't leave, he should leave."[63] During the eighteen-day uprising, Mubarak and his then–vice president, Omar Suleiman, agreed that "Egyptian youth" had revolted.[64] They also concluded that young Egyptians in general were agents for progress and change. On February

10, 2011, one day before Mubarak's abdication, Suleiman stated that "the January 25 youth movement has succeeded in pushing major change toward the path of democracy."[65] In doing so, he committed himself to protecting "the revolution of the youth."

January 25 and After: Old Wine in New Bottles

After Mubarak's fall on February 11, 2011, the Supreme Council of the Armed Forces (SCAF) took power in the interim, with old and new attitudes to youth, youth co-optation, and youth repression. The story of youth as hope versus youth as threat, however, remained the same. The framing of the SCAF and of subsequent regimes, however, and their policies toward young people became more distorted than that of any of the previous regimes. In the few months after Mubarak's ouster, the "radical" youth who had mobilized for this were sometimes referred to as the promise/hope when they were willing to be co-opted into the newly established political parties and the government bureaucracy. But when the youth groups mobilized for more demonstrations, as in November 2011 to support the families of people who had lost their lives during the January 25 uprising, they were referred to as the threat, and the media machine started to denounce them.

When Mohamed Morsi won the presidential elections in 2012, some of his support had come from young political activists together with certain public figures.[66] Nevertheless, he, too, perceived young people as either the hope or the threat. During his tenure, Morsi actively co-opted Islamist youth into the government bureaucracy, the pro-Islamist Freedom and Justice Party (FJP), and university clubs and unions. Young people from the liberal or leftist opposition were excluded from government positions and from higher political ranks in the bureaucracy. A few months after his election, demonstrations erupted against him in reaction to his Constitutional Declaration of November 2012, which awarded him extensive executive powers. Weekly protests followed until he was toppled by the military in 2013.[67]

Since Morsi's ouster, heavy-handed security has been the rule rather than the exception, with widespread arrests and detentions of university students accused of being members of the Muslim Brotherhood. In addition, hundreds of students have been suspended from their universities, while the government increased the fees for university dormitories in an attempt to reduce the number of students living there. The security apparatus has engaged with many clashes with students, who participated in demonstrations against the regime. During the 2013–2014 academic year, 1,352 students were arrested, and at least 10 students were killed on different public university campuses.

The Ministry of Higher Education issued new student regulations in 2014 that curtailed student civic and political participation on university campuses.[68] Contention between the regime and students heightened in February 2015, when the High Council of Universities dismantled student unions and banned student union elections. In al-Azhar University, for instance, the student union became defunct, and, as of the writing of this book, no elections have been held since 2013.[69] According to a former member of the student union at al-Azhar, "There are too many security concerns and too much censorship; many events are cancelled because the university is afraid of having too many young people in one place."[70]

The discourse on youth has also increased, and many policy objectives for youth issues have been publicized. The interim president, Adly Mansour, included a few youth figures in the Constitutional Committee of 50, which was entrusted with revising the 2012 constitution. This revision resulted in a "new" Egyptian constitution, which was adopted in 2014. According to its Article 82, "the state shall guarantee the provision of care to the youth and youngsters shall endeavor to discover their talents; develop their cultural, scientific, psychological, physical and creative abilities, encourage their engagement in group and volunteer activities and enable them to participate in public life." In addition, Article 180 states that "one quarter of the seats [of the Local Administration] shall be allocated to youth under thirty-five years of age." Article 244 announces that "the State shall endeavor that youth, Christians, persons with disability and Egyptians living abroad be appropriately represented in the first House of Representatives to be elected after the Constitution is approved, as regulated by law." In a public address to mark the new constitution, Mansour described youth "as pillars of the nation and progress." He claimed that "you [the youth] have been the fuel of the two popular revolutions. The phase of building and empowerment is still ahead of you. Build your future and participate in political life, through enriching partisan action. You should be sure that your efforts will bear fruit."[71]

Al-Sisi and Youth

Following Abdel Fattah al-Sisi's rise to the presidency in 2014, the elite discourse on Egyptian youth has broadly incorporated two main themes. First, al-Sisi communicated a conciliatory and somewhat apologetic message in September 2014 when he stated to young people in Egypt that he was "sorry to have neglected" them.[72] Second, he affirmed his desire for Egypt's youth to be on his side, and he promised young people that they would have more opportunities for political, social, and cultural inclusion through his state's new National Youth Council to improve the dialogue between government and youth.[73]

Al-Sisi's conciliatory discourse was inflected with much of the paternalistic vocabulary that had been present in the elite discourse under Mubarak. For instance, while addressing Cairo University students a few months after he became president in September 2014, al-Sisi addressed students as "sons and daughters." In addition, in articulating his love for Egypt's youth, he affirmed that he considered them "his children."[74] He also discussed young people's importance as productive forces in the national renewal of the economy. In urging Egyptian youth to help "build a new Egypt," al-Sisi has been explicit that in doing so, they must build with him. For instance, he stated, "I need your [Egyptian youth's] trust, I need your loyalty."[75] In this way, the president's message to Egyptian youth has been that you can become involved in "national projects" and governance, but only in particular ways; otherwise, "stay out of politics."[76]

The Renewed Dilemma of Youth as Both Threat and Hope

As a result of the mobilizational capabilities exhibited by young people in the four years following Mubarak's ouster, al-Sisi, as well as interim president Mansour, passed new laws and regulations in an attempt to end youth mobilization. In a parallel strategy, co-opting youth became important in showcasing youth inclusion in the polity. Immediately after the 2011 uprising, young activists were able to organize and express their opinions on campuses, and Egyptians generally regained their right to demonstrate.[77] Yet this culture of protest, which had emerged gradually in the decade preceding 2011, in large and significant street demonstrations about labor rights, human rights, and political freedoms, was heavily stifled from 2013 onward.[78] Under al-Sisi, the freedoms of association and assembly have been harshly restricted.[79] The "protest law" of 2013 mandated jail sentences for those who participated in any demonstration not approved by the Ministry of the Interior, as well as a minimum sentence of two years' imprisonment for an indeterminate range of offenses, including "violating public order."[80] This law enabled the regime to imprison tens of thousands of young activists for simply protesting. In addition, the new Terrorist Entities Law employs vague terminology "that can easily be applied to human rights advocates and peaceful political opponents."[81]

The Social Networks Security Hazard Monitoring Operation, announced in 2014, was an attempt to correct the perceived failings of previous strategies for crackdown on the public sphere by utilizing regular and mass surveillance of digital activity rather than individual cases of surveillance in specific investigations.[82] This legislative thrust was accompanied by a new discourse propagated by al-Sisi that underscores the purported "threat of the Internet" as a tool for terrorist groups to recruit members and obtain funding.[83]

With a handful of exceptions, the regime's efforts to control cyberspace before 2008 and up until 2014 were restricted to the prosecution of individual activists on the basis of their personal use of social media.[84] These prosecutions also depended on "spare legal provisions" in the Egyptian Penal Code, "principally designed to combat so-called 'publishing crimes.'"[85] The sentencing of blogger Karim Amer in 2007 to four years in prison, under the Mubarak regime, for insulting the president and Islam, marked the first targeting of an Egyptian citizen by the authorities on charges concerning online freedom of expression.[86]

Student demonstrations increased after the ousting of Morsi in July 2013, especially after the display of military and police brutality against Muslim Brotherhood protesters in August 2013, in what became known as the Rab'a Massacre.[87] Many student protesters were rounded up and imprisoned, and student unions were cancelled at public universities.[88]

Co-optation strategies have been reflected in other laws as well, such as Electoral Law 46/2014, which requires that electoral lists composed of fifteen members should include seven members from excluded groups, like women, Copts, and youth. Two of the seven should be youth. Electoral lists of forty-five candidates should include a higher number for each marginalized group, six of whom should be young people. Especially since his inauguration as president in 2014, al-Sisi announced more initiatives to co-opt a large number of the youth. In 2015 he established the Presidential Leadership Program (PLP). Its main objective was to develop young people's leadership skills in the social sciences, politics and security, and business management.[89] The program was under the direct control and sponsorship of the executive branch. Young people were given incentives to participate in it and to find employment after they had finished the fifteen-week program. In 2017, this program became more institutionalized and turned into an academy.[90] The regime has also sponsored a few conferences dedicated to young people. For instance, four youth conferences have been held during 2016 and 2017, all under al-Sisi's auspices. They all revolve around depoliticizing young people and directing them toward social, developmental, and entrepreneurship issues.[91] During a focus-group discussion, some participants spoke about an example at a conference that was held in Alexandria under the auspices of the Ministry of Youth, for the empowerment of young members of political parties. Typically, only young people who were "tolerated by the regime have been invited to this conference. . . . [I]f a young person is not within the sphere of a 'tolerated' opposition, and is considered by the security apparatus as posing a political threat, he is directly excluded from participating in political life."[92]

Conclusion

This chapter utilized the political economy of youth approach to analyze the macro structure of the polity, through shedding light on the national narratives and policies toward young people since the Free Officers seized power until today. During the past six decades, the subsequent regimes have tried to develop avenues for organized social and political participation under their control, in which they can co-opt the youth who are perceived as embodying the promise/hope of the nation. Young people who participate in these tolerable spheres are those who are interested in advancing social and political reform within the established red lines. They are also young people who are interested in advancing their own political careers within the system. On the other hand, repression has been widely used against young people who do not accept the status quo and who challenge the regime, either through protest movements or through mobilizing for demonstrations. These young people do not necessarily view themselves as a threat. They are sometimes the same young people who were working within the red lines, but they had found themselves to be beyond these established red lines due to policy changes. This was evident when the Nasserists, who were perceived as the hope during Nasser's era, turned into a threat against the nation when Sadat became president. The Islamists who were the threat under Nasser then turned into the hope with Sadat. The majority of politically and civically engaged youth do not choose to be a threat to the system, as will be discussed in the following chapters. They mostly turn to street contention and mobilization when political opportunities permit. Sometimes these opportunities erupt when extreme repression is utilized.

This chapter and the previous one have set the stage for understanding the macro structure of the political economy and the framing of young people by the different political regimes. The next three chapters discuss the agency of youth within this structure, how they perceive themselves, and how they have developed and accepted their own positioning in the polity.

3

Dilemmas of Civic and Political Engagement

Previous chapters discussed the political economy of youth approach within the context of Egypt. They demonstrated how the subsequent regimes from Nasser until today have developed a political economy in which authoritarianism, securitization, and neoliberalism persist. They also discussed the regimes' strategies and framing toward young people. Within this context, this chapter analyzes how young people deal with their positioning and how they perceive themselves within this system. What are the avenues in which they participate, and how do they act as agents of change and continuity? This chapter discusses the complexity and the dilemmas faced by young people who are civically and politically engaged. These youth accept the political economy of authoritarianism and work within its boundaries for social and political progress and reform. Thus, from the regime's perspective, they should be the hope of the nation as well as the main group of loyal young people.[1] However, while conducting fieldwork with these young people, it is evident that they are not passive actors within the boundaries of "loyal youth" or "hopeful future." They accept the grand narrative of neoliberalism, with its emphasis on individualism, youth empowerment, government–civil society partnership, the reform of the education system for an easy school-to-work transition, and a market-oriented capitalism. Nevertheless, they are critical of the regime's excessive corruption and are critical of the increased securitization of the public sphere. The majority of the interviewees have acted as if they accept the boundaries placed on them by the regime; however, when analyzed further it is evident that the respondents accept only the general global, neoliberal narrative and not that of the securitized, autocratic regime.[2]

The Fieldwork

Even though the Mubarak regime supported youth civic and political participation within the boundaries of the authoritarian, cleft capitalist system, youth participation in formal organizations has been scant at the national level. A number of empirical studies since 2011 have found that only 4.5 percent of young people in Egypt were members of humanitarian and charitable organizations, professional organizations, workers' unions, sports clubs, and scouting groups combined.[3] In this and subsequent chapters, I discuss the findings from the quantitative and qualitative data based on the Power2Youth (P2Y) research project. The quantitative analysis is taken from a random sample survey of 1,200 young people and was carried out in eight of Egypt's governorates between April 17, 2016, and May 10, 2016.

The qualitative analysis is based on thirty-three semistructured interviews and five focus groups with young civically and politically engaged people.[4]

The Promotion of Civil Society Organizations

As mentioned in chapter 2, the Mubarak regime supported the promotion of youth politics as part of the global neoliberal development policies. The Future Generation Foundation, spearheaded by Gamal Mubarak, in addition to the Ministry of Youth and Sports were the main venues within the boundaries of the authoritarian, securitized, neoliberal system for directing young people toward "organized" participation.

During the 1990s, scholars advocated for the promotion of civil society in authoritarian regimes in the hope of advancing democratization. The majority of studies concerned with this cite empirical evidence from Latin America and Eastern Europe.[5] The new millennium brought a new strand of literature, examining the extent to which civil society could have the opposite effect and thereby increase authoritarian resilience.[6]

It is argued that the two types of strategies employed by authoritarian regimes toward civil society actors are either a corporate strategy, in which
business associations, labor movements, nongovernmental organizations (NGOs), and charity groups are co-opted within state institutions;
or an exclusionist strategy, in which civil society actors are marginalized
from the development process.[7]

Other scholars have argued that civil society is a tool to promote neoliberalism. The erosion of the welfare state through decades of neoliberal
policies worldwide, especially in the developing world, established a new
global discourse, supported mainly by major international financial institutions (IFIs), like the World Bank and the International Monetary
Fund (IMF), in favor of civil society.[8] The rise of neoliberalism has disrupted social welfare and social protection provisions. To ensure the
sustainability of neoliberalism, IFIs have emphasized concepts of "'participatory development,' 'ownership,' consultation and 'social impact assessments.'"[9] New development policies put forward by the World Bank,
for instance, stipulated that civil society actors have to be consulted, in
addition to a country's government, before structural readjustment programs are implemented.[10] This strategy enabled NGOs to work hand
in hand with the IFIs and with the concerned governments to become
eligible for funding and to function "independently" of their respective
regimes. Hence civil society actors became an integral part of the IFI
conditionalities. It was considered that they would ensure transparency,
accountability, and good governance in authoritarian regimes.[11]

The Mubarak regime developed a corporate strategy in which it encouraged the establishment of civil society organizations, especially of
NGOs, and co-opted them into state developmental functions, while ensuring that they would not threaten the power of the regime. Many civil
society organizations were set up by entrepreneurs closely associated
with Mubarak and his family. Many others were established by individuals who were close to the political establishment or were themselves
politicians in it. The directors on the boards of a large number of civil

society organizations, for instance, were dominated by parliamentarians or government officials.[12] Blurring the line between state officials, the bureaucracy, members of the National Democratic Party (NDP), and civil society actors, especially NGOs, was essential to fill the welfare gap that the government was not fulfilling under the new IFI conditionalities. Civil society actors became important pillars on which the Mubarak regime relied for providing social services, especially healthcare and education. At the same time, civil society actors understood that for them to survive, it was essential to cooperate with the authoritarian regime and to deal with the state bureaucracy and its networks of privilege. This had the effect of reinforcing authoritarianism instead of promoting political liberalization.[13]

To maintain its dominance over the public sphere, the regime passed certain laws to restrict the independence of civil society actors. Among these, Law 84 in 2002 advocated political liberalization in the media, but its major provisions were devised to ensure the hegemony of the regime over social actors.[14]

In the post-Mubarak period, especially after al-Sisi's rise to power, the regime took a more security-conscious and exclusionist strategy toward civil society actors. The tighter security and militarizing of the polity showed the regime's determination to marginalize and exclude civil society actors from the public sphere. According to Mohamed al-Agaty, Law 70 in 2017, enacted under al-Sisi, is "the law of killing civil society" in Egypt.[15] It strictly controls the funding of NGOs, both foreign and domestic. The state authorities must be notified before any grants or funds from donors are received. The government also has the right to monitor the day-to-day activities of NGOs.

Since the Egyptian Economic Conference of 2015, which focused on entrepreneurship and was endorsed by al-Sisi, the regime has, however, been supportive of business startups, more so than NGOs. In 2017, for instance, another conference was held, under the slogan of *sherketak fekretak* (translated as "your company is your idea").[16]

The Promotion of Political Parties

In 2009, political party participation among young people was only 0.39 percent.[17] Of the former twenty-six political parties under the Mubarak regime, only two, the then-ruling National Democratic Party and the Democratic Front Party, contained youth divisions. In the two years following Mubarak's fall, twenty-nine new political parties were established. The majority of them included young people, while three of them—Masr al-Qaweya, al-Adl, and al-Dostour—were either established by the youth or had memberships that consisted more of youth than older people.[18] Young people who agreed to work within the authoritarian system were included in these small venues of formal participation in public life, while the rest were marginalized.[19] It is worth mentioning, however, that by 2016, once al-Sisi asserted his power, the state had disbanded almost all political parties. State security forces imprisoned a large number of the youth political party cadres, especially those who belonged to the more independent youth parties like al-Adl and Masr al-Qaweya. Our research team reached out to these party cadres, as the public sphere in 2015 had still permitted some fieldwork with political actors.

Who Are the Engaged Young People—the Hope?

When our fieldwork was conducted in 2015 and 2016, Law 70 had not yet been promulgated. The young people analyzed here as the hope, or as loyal, were still in the "Mubarak mode" of being co-opted by the regime with certain constraints. The closure of the public sphere by the al-Sisi regime, and its increasingly exclusionary policies toward civil society actors, was in its early stages. But as will be shown below, civically and politically engaged young people had already felt the regime's growing restrictions on civic and political participation.

According to the P2Y survey, only 3 percent of young people were members of civil society organizations. All of them were educated, with secondary or postsecondary degrees. Participation in civil society

TABLE 3.1 Answers to "Are You a Member in One or More Organizations?"

	"Yes" (%)	"No" (%)	Total (%)	N
Total	3	97	100	1,194
Basic education or less	0	100	100	456
Secondary education	3	97	100	497
Postsecondary education	7	93	100	241
Urban governorates	9	91	100	210
Lower Egypt	2	98	100	592
Upper Egypt	2	98	100	392
Above-average economic standard	12	88	100	96
Average economic standard	2	98	100	708
Below-average economic standard	2	98	100	390
Male	3	97	100	560
Female	3	97	100	634

organizations was associated with high education levels, more expensive places of residence, and high-income backgrounds. The more educated or the richer and more urban a young person is, the more likely he or she will participate in civil society organizations (table 3.1). This was confirmed during the qualitative fieldwork, when our research team had difficulty finding uneducated and low-income-level individuals in civic or political organizations. Consequently, nearly 90 percent of our young participants were middle class and educated. The survey shows that many of the engaged youth seem to be fairly passive members of civil society organizations, with 59 percent participating only a few times a year and 35 percent once a month. Internet activism was reported by 15 percent, and 10 percent said that they could become an internet activist in the near future. When asked whether they ever participated with a group of people to solve a community problem or to help others, 7 percent said they did, with the highest percentage again among postsecondary-educated young people (table 3.2).

During the qualitative fieldwork, the majority of participants stated that they were interested in civic and political participation to promote

TABLE 3.2 Answers to "Did You Ever Participate with a Group of People to Do Good or Solve a Problem in Your Community?"

	"Yes" (%)	"No" (%)	Total (%)	N
Total	7	93	100	1,194
Less than basic education	2	98	100	225
Preparatory/basic education	3	97	100	231
Secondary education	8	92	100	497
Postsecondary education	13	87	100	241
Male	9	91	100	560
Female	5	95	100	634

social, economic, and political change. Voting per se was not a priority, but participation to encourage socioeconomic change was. Many argued that during the past two years, young people had stopped their political participation due to the increasing security crackdowns on young activists. One respondent explained that "participation for me is mainly about being able to influence and change public opinions. This is not easy today."[20]

The survey did not ask young people whether they were members of political parties or social movements, because the Central Agency for Public Mobilization and Statistics—the institution that grants permission to conduct surveys in Egypt—did not permit certain "political" questions like these.

Although we have no data concerning participation in protest movements and political parties, our qualitative data indicated a similar relationship between education and participation. Only two informants in the semistructured interviews had less than secondary education. Another three had bachelor's degrees but earned only low incomes and lived in informal settlements. The regime's discourse in the aftermath of Mubarak's ouster from power had encouraged young people to participate politically through voting, while imposing constraints on other forms of civic participation. For example, in 2015 before the parliamentary elections, *Al-Ahram*—a publicly owned newspaper—ran various articles encouraging young people to participate, asserting that "participation is a religious and national duty."[21] Similarly, in 2018 prior to the presidential elections, a campaign entitled *Hansharek* (translated as "participate") called on young people to vote and to support al-Sisi for a second term.[22] The challenges faced by these engaged youth in a heavily securitized, neoliberal regime are discussed below.

Youth as Partners for Development?

Young people who work for or are members of civil society organizations and political parties have discussed the different dilemmas they are faced with. They demonstrated the complex impact of the political economy on young people in authoritarian regimes. On the one hand, they mostly accepted the neoliberal narrative of youth empowerment, education reform, and participation in civil society organizations, which is part of the global narrative of youth participation. However, on the other hand, they saw the contradictions of this system in relation to their own positioning in the polity. They also saw a disconnect between the regime's discourse on youth inclusion in the civic and political realms and its actions. They showed that working within the boundaries that the regime had established was not an easy task. There is a thin line between "tolerable" and "intolerable" activities, as perceived by the regime. For instance, one artist had established an independent organization to promote youth art (an apolitical organization); they then wanted to organize an arts carnival for other artists to join but was denied permission to do so. Another young man who wanted to develop an independent job fair for young people was also denied permission. Hence, here, the contradictions of the securitized, authoritarian, neoliberal system can be seen. On the one hand, the regime wanted young people to be depoliticized, and turn to apolitical activities, yet even these activities could turn into intolerable acts at certain moments in a country's transition process.

Over the past few decades, the international community, led by the IFIs, has advocated a development model that focuses on youth experiences, class, and gender, political, and economic change in addition to conflict. This model has also advanced the idea that young people's struggles emanate mainly from the failure of the education system to develop a smooth school-to-work transition. To tackle this main problem, education reform becomes imminent. This model also attempts to depoliticize civic participation and social interactions.[23] From this perspective, youth are promoted to be "partners" in the development process.[24]

Youth policies have also been at the heart of the international initiatives to promote the youth-for-development approach. The previous chapters discussed how the subsequent regimes put youth politics at the forefront of their policy initiatives, either through co-opting young people or through inculcation. During the fieldwork, when we asked young people whether they felt included in the political process, they argued that people in authority—whether those in authority were directors of organizations or of government institutions—tend to treat them like children. One interviewee, for instance, argued that the political elite and society at large looks at young people as "a bunch of children" who do not understand the problems faced by the government, which has to accomplish many other things besides thinking of how to include young people in governing processes.[25] Another public university student and union activist commented that the regime had addressed young people as "children" long before January 25. A young woman in North Sinai gave an example of her meeting with the minister of finance in 2013 to advocate for a large factory project connected to the development of North Sinai. She says that the minister talked to her as if he was talking to a child, although he did promise to help her with the paperwork for her project. However, he never granted permission for the project to start, and she argued that she "was not taken seriously."[26] To her this was an example of her being marginalized in the system, even though she was trying to support economic development in a marginalized area of the country.

Similarly, young artists in one of the focus groups stated that they faced social stigmas because most in Egyptian society did not consider art production to be a real profession. This puts Egyptian artists at a disadvantage when trying to display their artwork. The artists interviewed argued that the regime and society viewed young artists as people with "loose morals." One young man explained that people on the street made fun of him because he has long hair and wears unconventional clothes. Another pointed out, "We just want to be heard. . . . [W]e are trying to prove our existence and that is all."[27]

Avenues for Participation

As discussed in chapter 2, the Mubarak regime tolerated youth who showed an interest in socioeconomic development. In this neoliberal, cleft capitalist regime, social entrepreneurship, charity work, and NGOs were encouraged to exist under certain legal and corporate restrictions. The young people involved in these were encouraged to work within the regime's red lines to develop "partnerships" with the regime to promote development. Most of our sample had begun their civic and political engagement during the last few years of the Mubarak regime. They explained that the two years following Mubarak's ouster were important in establishing new venues and organizations for young people's civic and political participation, especially some that were concerned with youth issues.

During this two-year period, young people's self-perception changed, and they believed more in their own power and ability to reform their polity. They perceived themselves to be *a hope* for the development of the nation. Our research team was able to trace twenty-nine new political parties, protest movements, and initiatives that were created after 2011. Many young people developed initiatives such as Baheya, an organization established to promote women's rights. Others founded online news outlets like Mada Masr, to promote independent journalism, or political parties like al-Adl, to promote justice and inclusion of young people in the political process. Young people in these organizations believed in the importance of being in touch with other citizens, which required their presence "on the street." For these young people, "street work" was the most influential method of achieving reform. "Street work" in this sense is not necessarily demonstrations, but it also means reaching out to passersby through flyers about different issues, like women's rights. It also includes festivals that promote charity. Nevertheless, through increased security measures and militarization, the regime has been clamping down on young people's presence on the street, even if they are attempting to promote charity organizations.[28]

The main challenge faced by the majority of civically and politically engaged young people is, as they put it, the "shrinking of the public sphere" or the "shrinking of the street."[29] An interesting case is sports activities: ironically, sports were promoted by the Nasser regime as a main force for depoliticizing young people. Sadat and Mubarak also developed the Ministry of Youth and Sports to be the main institution to co-opt young people, while al-Sisi encouraged marathons as part of an initiative to promote public health. Nevertheless, when interviewing a young woman who developed an organization that promotes sports events in different Egyptian governorates, she explained, "I feel insecure, because I am always threatened by having to deal with security concerns and security closures of our marathons without prior notice."[30] In 2014 a 5K run was organized at the pyramids, and the night before the organizers received a phone call from a security official demanding that she cancel the event. The organizers met with various security peronnel with various security personnel to convince them that the run was apolitical and would not harm the public or threaten public security. After many meetings the security official agreed to supervise the run, but only on another day. Hence, the growing securitization of the public sphere constrains the work of young people who believe in the global neoliberal project and who also can work as forces for legitimating the regime.

Another young woman whose initiatives were about women's rights contends that "the public space is narrowing down; no one can work on the streets anymore."[31] She explained that her organization used to hold public gatherings or bring in experts to discuss films about gender equality; however, after June 2013 security became a concern for her and her colleagues: "We are afraid to put people under security investigations. You never know if the police will break into your organization and charge you with illegality or not."[32] Another young woman said that there is no due process of law to hold men in general and the security forces in particular accountable if they harass women, and this puts women under physical threat. She argued that even though there is an anti-harassment law, the police and policy makers do not enforce it, and that even the media indirectly sanction harassment against women. "The media talks about what a girl should and should not wear, so that men do not harass her. Why does the media look at the victim instead of trying to solve the problem?"[33]

Street carnivals are also beginning to experience security constraints. One carnival, which was organized by an NGO, was cancelled in 2014 because of security concerns. Another project, intended to bring in artists each month to present their work in front of Abdeen Palace in downtown Cairo, one of the president's official residences, and to influence social change from below, was also shut down by the regime.[34]

A young photographer stated that he stopped photographing news events, because it was no longer safe to do so. "Today we don't know what is right and what is wrong according to the laws and regulations, and I don't want to put myself in danger. I don't want to be a martyr; I can make a difference while I am alive through my photography."[35] A young man helping secondary school students to develop their extracurricular activities at public schools stated that there are "a lot of young people who believe that we could make a difference in Egypt. However, with recent events, they gave up, as no one is interested in developing new initiatives at all."[36]

It is clear that the al-Sisi regime has clamped down on the spaces for civic and political participation compared to the Mubarak era. This clamping down has been in response to the blooming of civil society for the two years that followed the 2011 uprising. As a consequence, many young people have chosen to exit the formal sphere, while others have turned to other spaces, mainly business startups and entrepreneurship.

More Entrepreneurial Philanthropy and Fewer NGOs

The global discourse on development has been in favor of developing connections among businesses, philanthropy, and national governments. Government–civil society and private business partnerships have been promoted by the regime as part of the promotion of civil society and development.[37] Entrepreneurial philanthropy has also been used by the regime as a means for development. This is to ensure that the private sector through private giving can fill the void that governments have left in social protection programs.[38] Entrepreneurial philanthropy refers to the pursuit of entrepreneurs to develop a basis of nonprofit social objectives through actively investing in the economic, cultural, and social resources in the country in which they live.[39]

This trend has also been followed in Egypt, where young people asserted that the current regime is supporting philanthropy organizations more than NGOs. Those in one focus group argued that promoting entrepreneurial philanthropy requires better education systems and more capacity-building courses to increase public education.[40] Yet they maintained that the current regime with its technocratic government talks about the importance of philanthropy, even while it passes restrictive laws that curtail the development of new companies. In this focus group, young people contended that a major problem with the government advocacy for philanthropy and entrepreneurship was that it addressed only affluent youth, who knew other languages and whose parents were sufficiently well-off to help them establish their private companies.[41] Another problem was that one of the government's initiatives, entitled Kadet al-Mustaqbal (future leaders), was organized by the then–prime minister, Ibrahim Mehleb, in August 2013. Like similar political initiatives, it was vague, established rapidly, and died off just as quickly. This particular initiative invited many businessmen to speak to young people about the importance of building new businesses, but as one focus-group participant observed: "No one really knows what they [the initiatives] are about, and there is no clear direction concerning the government's strategy. After a while the Kadet al-Mustaqbal initiative died out, since it was more about the trend of taking photos with young people and posting them on news outlets than about the initiative itself."[42] One young woman argued that the al-Sisi regime was trying to push youth away from political and NGO work and into entrepreneurial philanthropy. She contended that "what they [the regime] are trying to do is to decrease the number of young people who are active politically so they could say that young people who are interested in political participation are only a minority."[43] Another young man argued that the regime only allowed young people to engage in the areas where it wanted them to be, not in the areas where youth themselves wanted to be. Another issue of contention for civically engaged young people is that the regime puts pressure on them to try and find solutions for the country's social problems, without providing them with a legal or social infrastructure to solve these problems. "When we fail to solve some issues, like education problems, for instance, the regime interferes in our work to show that we as young people . . . cannot solve problems and are in need of the state to help us."[44]

Young people who were members of NGOs discussed the importance of bringing the state back into the infrastructure and welfare systems to help in the developmental process. "As long as the regime is stepping back from its duties in the welfare and in the enhancement of the education and health systems, young people cannot reform the country on their own."[45] Some young people argued that although the regime claims to empower young people to promote development and business initiatives, in reality it is constraining them.[46]

Only a fraction of young people in our sample, who work in entrepreneurial philanthropy and small business initiatives, believed that the regime had encouraged them in their work. One young entrepreneur who started a small business initiative stated,

> I was able to influence policy making concerning the technology and innovation center in Egypt, which is center right [leaning and] under the auspices of the Ministry of Communication. Now I have become a member of the board of directors, and the minister meets with us every month, and the government listens to our ideas a lot. I was also invited to attend the economic conference that was held in Sharm El Sheikh. . . . I was also provided with the opportunity to have a small talk with al-Sisi.[47]

The dilemmas of young people are important analytically when trying to understand the interplay between securitization, growing authoritarianism, and neoliberalism within a given regime. Even though the international community and the IFIs support the NGO-ization and depoliticization of youth to promote the global neoliberal project, in some instances this becomes challenging when authoritarian regimes are re-asserting their power. Young people who accept the NGO-ization, *and* their depoliticization, are faced with mounting pressures, repression, or threats of repression. The insecurity they felt while they engage civically in different apolitical events highlights the complexity of civic engagement in authoritarian regimes today. Many of the respondents' answers also showed that the regime's perception toward young engaged people had turned more toward securitization and threat, even if these same young people were hailed as the hope during the Mubarak regime and the early stages of the al-Sisi regime. Young people themselves on the other hand, especially those who are engaged in civil society organizations, do not perceive themselves as a threat to the nation, but rather as a hope for the future.

The Mirage of Political Engagement

Like in many other authoritarian regimes, political participation has been tricky in Egypt. Political parties have been tolerated since the Sadat regime and into the first few years of al-Sisi's ascendance to power. Political parties, however, as argued in the previous chapters, have had to acquiesce to authoritarian rule, without crossing red lines that were not tolerated by the regime. The dominant political party, the NDP in particular, was adept at co-opting young people to its ranks during the last decade of Mubarak's rule. During his short-lived presidency, Mohamed Morsi was adamant at co-opting young people, especially members of the Muslim Brotherhood, to the then-ruling Freedom and Justice Party (FJP).

In the few years between Mubarak's ouster and al-Sisi's ascendance to power, political parties increased, with many being established by young people who were members of protest movements during the Mubarak era. The P2Y fieldwork was conducted during a time of transformation, where political parties were already established and still existing in the public sphere. However, during the fieldwork the al-Sisi regime was slowly asserting its power and cracking down on political parties and their members, especially the young therein.

This chapter and the following two chapters capture the dynamics under which the politically engaged youth were functioning in the early part of the al-Sisi regime (2014–2016) and what young people's concerns were for the future. The increasing securitization and repression in the public sphere made it clear back then that they would have to stall their political engagement in the future. In hindsight, it is evident that youth political engagement in formal political parties other than Mostaqbal Watan (Nation's Future Party and a pro-al-Sisi regime party) has ceased to exist.

At the time of the fieldwork, young people who were members of political parties discussed how the al-Sisi regime portrays itself as including young people in decision-making, while it actually marginalizes them. One young member of a political party said,

> We were once invited to discuss a certain law with the minister of youth. After we sat down, he told us we are not here to discuss the law, we are here to discuss how we [the ministry] could help young people. Young people from different parties proposed to the minister that it should allow us as leaders from the youth wings in the parties to use the youth centers as forums to discuss political development issues. However, the minister contended that we cannot do this, since we are not allowed to politicize the youth centers.[48]

One young man stated that, since the June 2013 coup, he was no longer interested in participating politically and was instead interested in civic participation. He explained, "Currently I am unable to work within the political system, since political parties are not functioning. Until political parties are taken more seriously and until political party leadership develops its ranks, I am going to continue working in development. At the moment we cannot consider that the political parties we have in Egypt are 'real' political parties. . . . I feel that the entire system is flawed."[49]

A young man from an oppositon political party felt that the regime is indoctrinating young people who are interested in political participation with neoliberal and authoritarian ideas.[50] He said that some young members from his political party were invited to attend a conference held by the Ministry of Youth in Alexandria in 2015: "When they returned back, they were inculcated with different ideas than our own political party. . . . Now these young people's main interest is to fight the Muslim Brotherhood and to protect Egypt's national interest. . . . They also returned back believing that the regime should not disclose information concerning the military's involvement in the Yemen war, for national security purposes."[51]

Another young man in the same focus group said that he used to be a member of the Free Egyptians' Party, but in 2014 he switched his membership to the Mostaqbal Watan Party.[52] But he argued that as a young person he has very little impact on political proceedings in the party and on the national level. "We just have meetings, and these meetings do not result in anything; therefore I think it is more useful to work on developing young people's skills like teaching them how to have constructive dialogues with other people who are from different political ideologies, so that young people know how to discuss different ideas on common grounds."[53] The extent to which Mostaqbal Watan will move into being a dominant political party is still not clear at the time that I was writing this book. However, as argued earlier, during the parliamentary elections in 2020, it won 315 seats compared to 57 in the previous elections.[54] A dominant political party is an important force for co-opting young people and for adding to the durability of authoritarian regime.[55] The extent to which the al-Sisi regime will rely on political co-optation is still unclear, since the regime has relied heavily on securitization and repression as a means of durability.

The grievances discussed by young politically engaged people demonstrate the difference between the framing of the importance of youth in politics and the actual regime's policies of marginalizing these young people. For instance, Mostaqbal Watan was established by young people; however, as demonstrated earlier, these young people were pushed to the margins of the decision-making process within the party. Other analyses on Egyptian young people have also discussed the fact that young people have become vocal about calling for social and economic reform in addition to increasing freedom, justice, and social equality.[56]

Gender Struggles

The international trends of increasing the number and scope of NGOs have impacted feminist activism and civic participation. It is argued that by the end of the twentieth century, the majority of feminist activists worldwide changed their participatory modes from movements to NGOs. During the past two decades, engagement in these organizations has changed the relations between civil society and the state. NGOs have become arenas in which feminist struggles are played out and the development of new categories of gender relations and feminist identities have been developed.[57] State feminism has been advanced in Egypt since the beginning of the economic liberalization process with Sadat, and that increased with Mubarak. In the year 2000, for instance, the National Council for Women was established to enhance women's empowerment and to propose policies in favor of women's rights.[58] The promotion of women's rights and empowerment became tied with the regime. However, the ideas of "empowerment" are within the boundaries of a patriarchal society. A result of that was a pushback against the statist control of women's rights in Egypt and the efflorescence of women's organizations and the rise of a new generation of young women who engage to promote their rights.

The majority of young women in the sample tended to be active independently or in NGOs. Their main concern was to change social stigmas against women. They believed that the major locus for change lies not in the state, but in society. A young woman who works in an NGO and lives in an informal settlement summarized it this way:

> I wish I was free; I wish the person in front of me would trust my decisions and give me the same benefits as young men. I wish I would be able to travel; the family perception is always "how would you travel alone? You have to have someone to take care of you." Even if a girl finally gets married, she faces other sorts of problems. Why is it that if a man cheats on his wife, she has to accept it because she's a woman, while if it is the other way around, her husband would kill her, and it would be socially acceptable for him to do so? Even when both men and women do illegal things, the woman is treated unfairly. I wish I could change all of that.[59]

Another young woman argued that "the problem is that many people still believe that the girls are to blame for harassment, and this is very hard to change."[60] A major associated issue for young women was to change society's perception of the "right" age of women to get married, which was in their early twenties. An activist who developed an initiative for women's rights said, "I wish that a woman could say out loud that they don't want to get married before thirty-five. Our social perception needs to change."[61] She further argued that whenever she discusses women's rights, people interpret it from a religious perspective and turn feminism into antireligion.

Young women discussed their struggles within their families and in society at large. Some of them claimed that they were not able to go out with their friends as much as their brothers did, because their families were against young women going to cafés like young men did. Others, whose families allowed them to go out, faced different types of marginalization, such as not being able to drive alone at night out of fear of harassment. Another young woman contended that life in Upper Egypt was tougher on young women: "Girls really don't have the option of moving [alone on the streets or away from home] in Upper Egypt. It's not only in movies, it's in real life!"[62]

These discourses, especially concerning harassment, are skillfully promoted by the regime in order to control the extent to which young women have access to the public sphere. In 2011, for instance, a few months after Mubarak's ouster from office, al-Sisi was a member of the Supreme Council of the Armed Forces, which advocated forcing young women to undergo virginity tests. During a TV interview, al-Sisi admitted that the military had asked the police to hold virginity tests on young women who attended a sit-in at Tahrir Square.[63] He argued that these tests were essential to prove that these young women were not "virgins" and hence not worthy of respect. In addition, he stated that it would be proof that the military did not rape these young women, as some might have alleged.[64] In 2016, an Egyptian MP, Elhamy Ageena, called on the Ministry of Higher Education to enforce virginity tests against young girls before admitting them to a university.[65] This call was criticized by the director of the National Council for Women and by the president of Cairo University.[66]

According to Ruba Salih and her colleagues, women's rights and gender equality in the Middle East and North Africa (MENA) region are intertwined with state feminism. They state that "the legacy of these opportunistic forms of state feminism weighs on the capacity of local women's rights activists to promote inclusive public debates, notably due to the widespread perception of gender mainstreaming and women's rights agendas as being tied to the past authoritarian regimes, and against Islam and Islamist political opposition."[67]

These dilemmas are prevalent among young women who engage to enhance other young women's life chances and rights. However, they are still within the confinement of a patriarchal regime, which promotes only the rights that would contribute to the regime's self-interest. An example of which is increasing the number of female ministers or providing a quota for women in parliament. These numbers are window dressing for international legitimacy, but they do not intend to end the patriarchal system or to empower women.[68]

What Is Reform and Change for Young People?

As discussed earlier, civically and politically engaged young people mostly accept the neoliberal understanding of development. They rarely see a problem with the general narrative around it, because they want to work and develop within such a system. The majority of informants believed that change meant new policies for sustainable development, as well as economic and political reforms. All the young people in our sample, irrespective of background, concluded that two major factors were necessary for positive change in Egypt: the due process of law, and education reform.[69]

Some young people, primarily members of NGOs, argued that development could only be achieved if the regime enacted serious legislative reforms. They also said that the regime should trust civil society actors and give them more freedoms and access to the "streets." They were convinced that they, as part of civil society, could help in the process of change and development. Nevertheless, this alone was not sufficient because more resources for development should be provided by the regime. The problem, however, was that they believed the regime was not willing to change. Corruption and nepotism were embedded in society, and the regime was not keen to change that.[70]

The respondents therefore were developing their own initiatives to make small-scale changes. For example, a young man who is a member of a private university student union argued, "Today my main job is to change my own community and university, because if this changes, the whole country could change."[71] A young woman who works in a community development NGO based in an informal settlement said, "Through my work here at the NGO I teach children in my community to become more responsible and more educated people, to help change this community for the better. However, I can't do that on my own; the state should also engage in this process through investing more in education."[72]

Some young people have argued that it is easier for them to reform their polity by becoming an integral part of the regime, instead of trying to work outside it. A young lady from Aswan explained that in 2010 she wanted to develop an initiative in her hometown to clean the streets. However, she could not succeed on her own, and the only way she could do it was through joining the NDP branch in Aswan. Another young woman who worked in a large charity organization commented,

> Since I started to work at this NGO, I realized that NGOs are very easily corrupted and penetrated by the state. Since the current regime is interested in "innovation" and "philanthropy" the NGO I work at has changed its work to cater to this. . . . The government sponsors this organization to use and abuse it; it tells the organization to do certain projects and I don't like this, and no one is interested to change in my opinion.[73]

Another young member of an NGO said that he lost hope for reform after the January uprising. He said, "Now I feel that all my freedoms and rights were taken away from me all of a sudden."[74]

It is evident from young people's aspirations and perceptions of change and development that there is a duality and complex relation between the dilemmas of living and engaging in a securitized, neoliberal, authoritarian system. Here young people display their disaffection with the increased securitization and repression. They also blame corruption and nepotism for the social and economic problems. However, they do not criticize the neoliberal model or discourse of youth depoliticization or youth empowerment per se. They believe in the importance of empowering young people's capacity to become more competitive in the market economy. For instance, a member of a public university student union argued that his main goal was to create an easy school-to-work transition for his fellow students. The union established an activity that helps young people in developing their own small businesses. They facilitate internships for students in different organizations and businesses and then make these businesses help them out in establishing their small businesses.[75] The general global discourse was encouraging youth to volunteer in charity organizations to achieve their goals and potential for a better society.[76] Hence the positionality of youth does not go beyond the global understanding of youth empowerment for development. Yet the youth perceive that corruption and securitization are impeding this process. Thus they engage within the current securitized, neoliberal system to promote the international neoliberal version of youth empowerment and economic development.

Conclusion

This chapter analyzed the dynamics of civic and political engagement of young people within the confines of an authoritarian, securitized, neoliberal regime. During the first decade of the 2000s, the Mubarak regime laid the groundwork for a plethora of civil society organizations, but only within its red lines. Since then, the al-Sisi regime has been imposing more restrictions on civil society actors. However, to comply with the IFIs' insistence on opening up the public sphere to civil society actors, the regime endorses philanthropic and business initiatives, while closing the sphere for increased youth civic and political engagement. The developmental work in areas, specifically health and education, in which young people are civically engaged has been tolerated as long as that work remained within small communities. However, the avenues for youth civic and political participation are constrained. Young people are not permitted to develop any initiatives in public places, even in the form of festivals, to advertise their organizations or as public awareness campaigns. Nevertheless, within this context they continue to show some optimism and hope for change. They believe in their ability to develop their own initiatives and organizations. Time and time again they have asserted their capability for enhancing change and for establishing their own parallel universe in which they can prevail. The regime's rhetoric promotes its image in the media as encouraging young people to become part of the governing structure. Prior to the 2015 parliamentary elections, for instance, a quota for "youth" was announced, to demonstrate the regime's pro-youth policies.

Even though the young people in this chapter represent young people who should be representatives of hope and loyalty for the regime, these same young people also discussed their marginalization and alienation in the polity. The regime itself is moving more toward a securitization discourse against these same young people, who were believed to be the hope under Mubarak and in the first few years after the uprising. Young people's thoughts, beliefs, and experiences in this system demonstrate that these "loyal" young people can quickly "exit" or "voice" their discontent of the system. This could lead to a situation where the options of exit and voice are both present, but young people choose to exit. Instead of becoming civically and politically engaged, they could disengage from public life altogether. Nevertheless, if these young people do not find a better alternative, and their exit is not sufficient, they would probably decide to voice their discontent against the regime. Some of the loyalists who have voiced their discontent have become part of the threat to the nation, and they are the subject of the next chapter.

4

Young Political Activists

A Threat to the Nation?

The decade preceding the Egyptian uprising of January 25, 2011, witnessed an increase in political opposition and activism against the Mubarak regime. Youth movements increased in number and scope from 2004, when the Kifaya movement emerged, until Mubarak's ouster.[1] The eighteen-day uprising against Mubarak revealed important dynamics about the impact of youth activism on political change. First, youth activists were adept at mobilizing citizens, and second, their ability to sustain street contention influenced the ending of the Mubarak regime. Youth mobilization strategies paved the way for the "Day of Wrath" on January 25, 2011. In addition to the large numbers of protesters in Tahrir Square, further mobilization took place in other major Egyptian cities like Port Said. The police stormed these events and increased the use of tear gas to control them. Nevertheless, young activists were able to revive their campaign and call for a "Friday of Anger," when they escalated demonstrations and demanded that Mubarak step down from power. On January 28 protesters marched en masse to Tahrir Square calling for the end of the Mubarak regime: "The sheer number of marchers overwhelmed the Ministry of Interior. In dramatic scenes, the police retreated from bridges and intersections."[2]

The mere fact that young activists were able to mobilize large numbers of people against an incumbent regime is important for making the regime feel fragile vis-à-vis activism and mobilization. The global securitized discourse toward young people, as being prone to political upheavals, civil wars, and terrorism, has also supported this discourse in the context of Egypt. Since the ouster of Mubarak, different strategies have been enacted to eliminate political activism. This chapter analyzes these strategies and their impact on young activists today. Here I zoom in on young political activists from the fieldwork's sample. These young people are important analytically, because they are perceived as a threat to the nation from the regime's perspective. The main task here is to understand the impact of today's securitized, neoliberal system on the life experiences of these young people. How do they navigate the spaces that are available to them and how do they participate in the polity? What are their perceptions of political change?

Mobilization and Contention after January 25

Street contention continued for two weeks after the 25th, with the military taking over streets to block demonstrations. Putting a stop to the protests was the primary military objective. When it became clear that contention on the streets would not subside, the Supreme Council of the Armed Forces (SCAF) pushed Mubarak to abdicate and decided to oversee the transitional process. Although the army's intervention was essential for Mubarak's downfall, its leadership was aware that "the public had induced a leadership transition."[3] During the interim years between Mubarak and al-Sisi, the army was the main actor in political life, even after Mohamed Morsi was elected president.[4] Led by the SCAF, the military secured many rights through the 2012 constitution, especially the right to keep the military budget beyond the oversight of state institutions.[5] However, when public outrage against Morsi escalated because of his authoritarian reversals, the military decided to depose him a year after he became president. According to some accounts, Morsi was seen as a national security threat to the military when he publicly supported various international jihadi groups.[6] Although neither Mubarak nor Morsi would have been ousted without the army's intervention, the military leadership continues to perceive political activism as a threat because of activists' ability to mobilize large numbers of demonstrators onto the streets.

The al-Sisi regime devised three strategies to offset the mobilizational capacities of youth opposition movements. The first strategy is the co-optation of some political activists through providing them with bureaucratic jobs and ministerial positions. It also announced a quota system for young people to become members of parliament. The second strategy is building a securitized media machine that defames and delegitimizes young political activists. This strategy was important in stirring public opinion against youth activists, especially during the first year of regime formation. The last and most important strategy is repression in order to stop political mobilization.

Regime Strategies against Young Activists

The first strategy, co-optation, entails a political exchange of rewards from the authoritarian leader in return for the acquiescence of oppositionists. This frequently turns into a patronage system, where the distribution of benefits is in monetary form or through the awarding of positions of power in state institutions.[7] These patronage systems enable dictators to exert control over those who receive the benefits and over those who become incorporated in the political process, even if they are in the opposition. Co-optation has been utilized by Egypt's authoritarian rulers, toward different opposition groups ranging from leftists to liberals and Islamists.[8]

The second strategy is developing the hegemony of a security-led mass media to defame young activists. The role of the mass media in autocracies to influence and manipulate citizens has long been addressed in the literature. The mass media have been a powerful tool for totalitarian regimes to control their populations.[9] In modern authoritarian regimes, the media have served incumbent regimes as instruments of propaganda. In China, for instance, the role of the media has been significant in legitimating the regime. It seems that China's citizens have supported their authoritarian regime largely as a result of media propaganda, while minimizing their own negative experiences with the government.[10] In Brazil, a study showed that public opinion under the military dictatorship reflected the ruling elite's discourse at the time, rather than citizens' own interests.[11] Thus, citizens' support of an incumbent authoritarian regime is largely dependent on whether they are exposed to media messages advocating the regime's policies.[12] It is evident that the media can be a major force in legitimizing an authoritarian regime and in fending off opposition to it.[13] In Egypt, the media have been utilized not only to legitimize the regime, but also to turn public opinion against young political activists.[14]

The third strategy is increased repression against young activists. A regime's perception of threat from contentious manifestations determines the "repertoires of suppression" that it will devise to exert social and political control.[15] The forms of repression range from direct to indirect. Some sanctions impose a physical cost on individuals and activists perceived as a threat, to deter them from engaging in certain activities. Direct forms of repression include torture, using physical force against an individual, or causing someone's disappearance or execution. Indirect forms of repression are banning political parties, using informants against dissenters, censoring newspapers, and arresting prominent activists.[16] The purpose of repression is both to stop protests forcibly and to deter activists from particular activities that are perceived by the regime to be challenging.[17] A regime's response to opposition is defined, first, by whether a certain group's actions are deemed unacceptable (for instance, in their number of challengers, their duration in the public sphere, and their geographic range); and second, by whether the group's beliefs, objectives, and relationship with the power structure in society are considered acceptable.[18] Although these repressive measures have strongly deterred political activism today, they also demonstrated the regime's reaction to the power and ability of these movements to cause political crises for Mubarak, the SCAF, and Morsi. Youth mobilizational strategies and protests were essential in bringing down Mubarak in 2011. They were also effective in creating a political threat to Morsi, which started with demonstrations against his November 2012 announcement to amend the then newly enacted constitution, and that ended in the successful military coup of 2013.

Young Activists

The concept of a young activist refers to all forms of political participation, whether formal or informal. An activist is a person whose main concern is to influence policies through traditional representations, such as becoming members in a political party, contacting politicians, campaigning on certain issues, or participating in voluntary organizations and nongovernmental organizations (NGOs).[19] Activism also refers to an individual's attempts to change the political system from outside it, such as participating in demonstrations, signing petitions, or boycotting certain products, as well as online attempts to influence politics and policies (for example, through blog posts).[20] In this chapter I focus on activists whose main repertoires are to influence the public sphere through demonstrations, sit-ins, and petitions. Young people discussed in this chapter come within the regime's perception of a threat to the nation. They are the youth who have decided to "voice" their discontent against the regime through various forms of activism. They are either independent activists protesting against regime policies; members of human rights organizations; former members of the Muslim Brotherhood; activists in protest movements; or activists in student unions who have mobilized against either the university administration or the regime. Even though these young people are from the same sample as the young people analyzed in the previous chapter, I discuss them separately here. These young people's activities have depended largely on political mobilization and contestation, unlike the rest of the sample whose civic and political engagement has mainly been through formal organizations.[21]

As discussed in the previous chapter, political questions were not allowed in the survey questionnaire; hence, we could not discern the exact numbers of young people belonging to protest movements or

TABLE 4.1 Answers to "Have You Ever Been an Internet Activist?"

	"Yes" (%)	"Never, but might become one" (%)	"No" (%)	Total (%)	N
Total	15	10	75	100	1,189
Less than basic education	4	7	89	100	223
Preparatory/basic education	14	12	74	100	228
Secondary education	14	10	76	100	497
Postsecondary education	29	13	58	100	249
Male	18	10	72	100	559
Female	13	11	76	100	630

opposition political parties, or who were merely independent activists. Nevertheless, we were permitted to ask whether young people were online activists or not. The survey results show that only 15 percent of young people are internet activists, with young people with better education standards being more likely to mobilize others online. Twenty-nine percent of highly educated people said they had been an internet activist before (table 4.1). This low percentage of online participation shows that social networking and information and communications technologies are indeed important in mobilizing for dissent; nevertheless, young people's presence on the street and in public spheres was perceived as being more threatening than online activism. In our qualitative fieldwork, young people discussed their life experiences on the streets and in public spheres more thoroughly than they did about their online participation.

Co-optation, as we have seen, is a key strategy used by authoritarian rulers to ensure loyalty among citizens, even some of the opposition. Many young activists are aware of these strategies and perceive them to be impeding their goals. It is also important to point out the fact that co-optation of young activists leads to movement fragmentation.[22] A young protest-movement activist commented, "Today the regime got rid of the various types of political activists. It created a rift between them: those who were willing to be co-opted are in enmity with those who are not, the first are marginalized, and the second are imprisoned."[23] In a similar vein, a young activist who was a member of a political party, and later of a political movement, commented that the state was adept at undermining young political activists who belonged to the opposition. He put forward an interesting argument about Shabab Jabhet al-Inkaz (or "The Rescue Front Youth").

This Front was composed of young people who were part of the April 6 Youth Movement and were ousted by its members. The Front's leader, Tarek al-Kholy, had been exploited by the state, which gave him airtime in media outlets to vehemently attack the April 6 Youth Movement. However, according to our interviewee, the state used al-Kholy only as a "picture" of being interested in including young people in the policy-making process. In reality, they marginalized him and excluded him from the governing process. Another example is that of Khaled Telema, who served as deputy youth minister after the events of June 30. When he came into conflict with the minister, the president got rid of Telema, and then all young deputies to ministers were dismissed. "He [al-Sisi] does not even include his own people, he only takes 'selfies' with them."[24]

Similarly, a focus-group participant explained that in 2014 a mock youth parliament was established by the Ministry of Youth.[25] It was a simulation in which young people participated as parliamentarians. The invitees did not include youth who belonged to nontolerated opposition parties like Masr al-Horreya and Masr al-Qaweya and al-Wasat, which some of our interviewees had belonged to. These young people believed that if a young person was not within the sphere of a "tolerated" opposition, then he or she was considered a security threat by the regime.[26] Young activists believe those who become co-opted by the regime are marginalized in the decision-making process. "If you are invited to any government-led event or if you work with the regime, you have no impact on the policy making level. . . . [T]hose who are in the opposition are excluded while those who are co-opted are marginalized."[27]

It is clear that the regime utilizes co-optation strategies that are capable of fragmenting youth movements. These strategies do work with

many politically engaged young people, as we saw in the previous chapter and as the activists in our sample themselves had been implying.
However, one important aspect of the weakness of this strategy under
the al-Sisi regime is that some young activists were skeptical of these
measures and saw them as marginalization rather than co-optation.[28]

The Activism-Media Nexus

The role of the media has been crucial in delegitimizing young political
and oppositional activists in the public realm. Studies on other authoritarian regimes like China and Russia have confirmed the importance of
the media in the process of authoritarian consolidation. Authoritarian
regimes are adept at using the media to stabilize their regimes and to
influence citizens' attitudes and behavior in their favor.[29]

The media's portrayal of young activists as terrorists or anarchists has
undermined society's perception of youth activists in the public sphere.
Young activists have also argued that the mere exclusion or blocking of
media outlets to opposition makes it even harder for them to have a better image in society.

Some young activists raised the example of a media campaign intended to tarnish the reputation of human rights activists. They explained that the media management did not provide human rights
actors with airtime or with space in mainstream newspapers to promote
their causes. Furthermore, it undermined them and portrayed them as
agents of the West. One activist, who previously belonged to the Youth
for Change movement, said that in 2010 he was able to visit informal settlements and collect signatures from the inhabitants to call on the gov-
ernor to develop access to basic goods in these areas. He explained that

> today this is not possible, due to violence and the media campaigns
> against activists. Citizens who used to sympathize with young activists no
> longer do so today. . . . I used to be able to go to informal settlements and
> discuss issues of injustice and political marginalization with inhabitants;

I used to mobilize people there to sign petitions. However, today I do not even attempt to enter these informal areas anymore, since exactly the same citizens who used to listen to me would [now] call the police and try to imprison me.[30]

An Ultras White Knight member argued that the regime's discourse and media machine have aroused political as well as social contempt for political activists. "The government developed a new public discourse against all youth, making the society against youth activists."[31] Media in this sense are not only influential in delegitimizing and tarnishing the reputation of young activists, but are also an important vehicle for inciting citizens against young activists. Many activists are afraid of the fact that their fellow citizens would report them to the police. During our fieldwork this was evident, when more than five activists did not want to hold the interviews in public spaces, especially in cafés. We had one incident where a young activist who was being interviewed stepped out from an interview when the café table nearby became crowded with strangers. This pattern is also seen in public opinion formation in authoritarian regimes such as Latin American military dictatorships. In Brazil, for instance, public opinion reflected the elite discourse at the time. At the height of the military dictatorship in 1972–1973, public opinion surveys showed that the majority of respondents were in favor of military intervention and supported the authoritarian policies.[32]

The Activism-Repression Nexus

The Mubarak regime employed a policy of "ignoring" some protest activities, which fueled a mobilization of labor movements with new collective identities.[33] The al-Sisi regime, on the other hand, has utilized a policy of repression against political activists. This has prompted new forms of contention that have become "shorter, localized, and more nimble."[34] In the wake of the Arab uprisings, Arab regimes have markedly increased their violence against citizens. In Egypt there has been a rise in civilian cases in military courts and a surge in jail sentences against activists and in the use of violence against demonstrators, often leading to hundreds of civilian deaths.[35] Three events in the immediate aftermath of the uprisings marked the increase in regime repression against protesters: the Republican Guard Massacre, the Nasr Street clashes, and the raids on protesters in Rab'a and Al-Nahda squares.[36] This not only was a manifestation of brute force by an authoritarian regime or its security forces, but also was an act of performative violence, which showed a ruthless willingness by a newly established regime to use force.[37] The state-backed media machine has overwhelmingly supported this repressive campaign, calling on the regime to protect the nation from the Muslim Brotherhood's intrusions.[38] The rulers since Mubarak and in particular the al-Sisi regime have "hoped to gain popular support by offering the promise of restored security and protection against both a growing domestic state of lawlessness . . . internal enemies in the form of the MB [Muslim Brotherhood] and jihadi groups, and the threat of external political intervention from neighboring countries and foreign powers."[39] Young people who mobilize for public demonstrations, call for the protection of human rights, demand political reform, or demonstrate in favor of the Brotherhood have been actively excluded from public participation by the regime. The regime developed preemptive strategies to prevent or deter them from political participation, and it also outlawed political opposition. Its main target has been the Brotherhood, but also in its sights were young political activists, in particular members of protest movements that were instrumental in the January 25 uprising, such as the April 6 Youth Movement.

The repertoires of contention, specifically street demonstrations, graffiti, and public awareness campaigns, coalesced into a political threat to the regime, which perceived them as having a large influence on public opinion. The regime's perception of these activists stemmed from its conviction that their calls for demonstrations and sit-ins, and their ability to mobilize the public in major cities, were unacceptable for public order and threatened the regime's survival. In addition, these activists' beliefs and objectives about reforming the authoritarian system and pri-oritizing social justice were anathema to the regime. Hence, immedi-ately after the Rab'a Massacre in 2013, the regime cracked down on youth participation. One youth organizer said, "Now we just froze, because of the security issues and the political situation which threatens youth activists. In addition, I am not interested in political participation any-more. People have either been jailed or had their reputation tarnished by the media."[40]

The case of the Muslim Brotherhood youth illustrates these dynam-ics, especially after the Rab'a Massacre. For instance, the movement en-couraged its young members to become active on university campuses to keep the "revolutionary activism" (al-hirak al-thawry). They built on that through developing an umbrella network of Brotherhood members and other activists entitled Students against the Coup.[41] The regime responded with another wave of repression and increased securitiza-tion. Security forces were deployed to all public university campuses. In addition, the state media described these young people as "thugs" who wanted to create chaos on university campuses.[42]

The Ultras youth groups (Egyptian football fans), which had mobi-lized against Mubarak, became empowered after his downfall through the graffiti they painted against the SCAF and by their chanting and demonstrating against the police and the state security apparatus. Nev-ertheless, after many demonstrations and encounters with the police during a few matches, they were outlawed. One consequence has been that members of the Ultras are afraid to demonstrate: "We gave up the streets, because if you go to the street you will get arrested again."[43] "The regime is at enmity with young people today, whoever is not pro the authority is either imprisoned or killed. . . . Therefore I am frus-trated and am not even interested in becoming politically active any-more."[44] This same activist further argued that members of the Ultras have been killed during many demonstrations: "whoever did not die, is now imprisoned."[45]

A young man who had participated politically both before and after January 25 commented,

> We used to be able to sit down and discuss politics. We discussed our dreams and goals. Today, all this is banned. People like us who are against al-Sisi and against the Brotherhood are very few. However, we are still harassed by the police force. Young people from April 6, Youth for Justice and Freedom, the Revolutionary Socialists, and some young people from al-Dostour Party know one another, but they cannot be effective because of security concerns. What is happening today against young opposition did not happen even during Nasser's era. We cannot hold any meetings, we cannot coordinate. Today if we meet, we are afraid of imprisonment, so we rarely meet.[46]

Young activists agreed that youth political participation today is totally banned, which makes them afraid even to discuss politics among their friends. One young man explained that today he does not talk about his political and security concerns with his friends or in cafés, even though prior to the January 25 uprising and in its immediate aftermath he used to discuss political matters everywhere. Now, however, he was afraid, as he could be jailed just for talking about such topics.[47] Another young man who was a member of a protest movement summarized how young political activists feel: "There is too much violence against young activists; my friends are imprisoned and people do not care for justice to prevail."[48] "I feel that all my freedoms and rights were all of a sudden taken away. So now I became afraid to work in the public space. I have a lot of fear."[49]

A young activist who discussed graffiti art argued that this was not considered a threat by the state, and no harassment against graffiti artists had ever taken place except after the events of November 2011, when graffiti artists began painting pictures of their deceased friends.[50] "Then the state started harassment, when they saw that passersby were watching this art, and were influenced by it."[51]

Another focus-group participant observed that "what they [the regime] are trying to do is decrease the number of all the people who are active politically so they can say that young people who are in the opposition are only a 'minority' of young people in general."[52] A young activist explained that the state imposed legal restrictions on the work of human rights organizations—to control their power and to limit their capacity to hold the state accountable for its human rights abuses. An independent activist explained, "I have many friends who are migrating on a regular basis, and this is something that makes the current regime happy—as it becomes easier to control the activists who are left behind."[53]

Another issue faced by some activists was problems at work. An opposition political party member who worked at a bank in downtown Cairo said that his boss had had a long chat with him in 2014, telling him to "eliminate political activism, since it is inappropriate to discuss politics at work. . . . After this discussion I was moved to another branch in New Cairo. . . . I did not lose my job, but it was a type of soft warning."[54] Another activist from the April 6 Youth Movement's Democracy Front claimed that he could not find a job: "as a young man in opposition, I cannot find a job, and someone else who is less competent than me got the job I applied for."[55]

Repression in the cases of these young activists has instilled many emotions among young activists, the most common of which is fear. This fear develops in self-policing and self-censorship among young activists, adding to demobilization. However, some studies have shown that fear and self-policing can sometimes trigger violence and clandestine activities, since some activists can become radicalized.[56] Thus young activists may be developing different coping strategies in the short term, but in the long term there could be an increase in radicalization and the use of violence.

Repression against University Activists

Youth activists from different protest movements and opposition parties were active on university campuses, especially in holding public events to promote a parliamentary or presidential candidate for the 2011 and 2012 elections. They also became adept at mobilizing and demonstrating for their own rights and freedoms of expression on campus. Today, however, these young activists are repressed by the security apparatus and are unable to demonstrate or to participate in public events.[57]

Some focus-group participants argued that even the free space in universities is being closed off to political activism. There were many cases of security personnel preventing young people from joining student unions (SUs) or simulation models. A young woman who was a member of the SU in a public university explained that "the authorities tell you that you are allowed to do whatever you want on campus, but then when it comes to certain activities or when it comes to listening to people from the opposition, they deny you this right for 'security concerns.'"[58] She contends that SU members had once invited former presidential candidates to speak on campus, but the security forces no longer granted them permission. In Cairo University, no Muslim Brotherhood supporter is allowed to be part of the SU or to participate in activities such as capacity-building workshops. Another young man, a member of a public university said that there was too much interference and censorship over SU activities. "Before 2013, we were allowed to hold any activity without security permissions, but now, we as a student union are not even allowed to initiate any events, if we want to hold any event, even if it is cultural, not political, it has to be under the umbrella of the faculty, not students. Sometimes permission for that is not even granted."[59] At a public university, for instance, student activists organized a sit-in and mobilized almost 300 other students to call on the university administration to pressure the regime to end the detention of their fellow students. However, the university security cracked down on all those who were part of the sit-in.

Repression is also used against SU members of private universities. For instance, when the SU of a private university in Cairo mobilized for a sit-in in favor of young people who were killed in Port Said in 2012, the university was shut for two weeks. Both the university security and the state security interfered to stop the mobilization process.[60] In addition, the administrations sent warning emails to all participating students' parents to convince them to stop the sit-in or else their children would be expelled.

In another sit-in that was conducted at the same university in 2014, after a student was killed by a car accident on campus, these same students were harassed by state security personnel through direct phone calls on their personal mobile phones. Forty students were expelled as a consequence of their protest.

Indirect repression is also used against students through various means like forcing parents to stop their sons and daughters from their protest activities. Or closing the job market against young activists, or denying them employment opportunities, or threatening to expel them from work or university. These intimidation policies are part of the mounting repression against activists. Activists have reacted to these different repressive measures through different means. They have either decided to disengage from political activism altogether, resort to other forms of engagement (mainly civic engagement), or develop what they call a "parallel universe" where they can discuss contentious issues or act politically beyond the formal political sphere.[61]

The Consequences of the Regime's Strategies
Political Disengagement

The al-Sisi regime's strategies of delegitimizing, co-opting, and repressing young political activists have reduced the interest of many young people toward political participation. In addition to the regime's control of the media, these repressive practices have impacted the way in which young people perceive the regime and how they engage. Many have argued that in recent years young people have chosen to end their political activism because of these strategies. One young woman, who had been an independent observer at the presidential elections in 2012, said that she was no longer interested in politics or activism.[62] She believed that since 2012 the security apparatus had been eavesdropping on her. Some of her colleagues had been sent to prison, or their reputations were demolished in the media.

A former protest-movement member said that he stopped his activism because of security threats against him. He was also not interested in participating in civil society organizations, as "they are being paid by the government today, they make contracts with the governments, to be protected."[63] Another former protest movement activist stated, "Today I am frustrated, if I go to a poor person to try to help him and tell him that the government is not conducting policies to protect the poor, instead of appreciating this, this person tries to report me to the police. Thus I am not even interested in being politically active anymore."[64]

Some young Brotherhood members have also shown restraint and abstention from political participation as a result of the current political repression and co-optation measures. "The high cost of protesting and political participation coupled with frustration over the Brotherhood's incapable leadership disenchanted several members who not only broke ties with the Brotherhood but also with politics as a whole."[65] Nevertheless, it is important to note that in the case of the Brotherhood youth in particular, political abstention is only one of different reactions to regime repression. Some activists have been adamant at having their "revenge" on the regime through using violence against the regime.[66] As argued previously, repression can have an adverse effect, where young people could become more radicalized as a consequence.

From Activism to Civic Engagement

Since the public sphere is closed for young activists, some have decided to move from political activism toward civic engagement. For instance, one SU activist who had mobilized against the securitization and imprisonment of his fellow students, decided to change his work from "political" issues to networking with organizations like Injaz, to help students in their school-to-work transition.[67]

Another human rights activist developed an initiative to change a space in downtown Cairo from being a garbage dump to a big playground where children and young people could go and do sports activities. Nevertheless, he argued that "the government brought a legal loophole to shut down this space."[68] A young feminist activist argued that she is no longer interested in street activism and is now part of a larger Arab feminist network that is concerned with changing the public discourse on women in the region. The network developed a Facebook campaign entitled "Hal Ta'lameen" (do you know) on learning about Arab constitutions and understanding all articles that are against women's rights.[69]

These coping mechanisms shed light on the relation between engagement in civil society organizations and political activism. As I argued in the previous chapter, authoritarian resilience theories contend that civil society contributes to the longevity of authoritarian regimes. Nevertheless, young activists' navigation from political activism to civil society is worth more analysis, since it seems from the respondents in this research that some young activists resort to civil society when the political context does not permit activism. However, once a political opportunity erupts, these same young people can revert back to their activism.

Developing "Parallel" Organizations

Some young activists, mostly university activists, have contended that they develop a "parallel" universe where they can voice their own opinions without any crackdown from the university administration or state security. This strategy was first developed under the Mubarak regime. During the 2000s, a parallel SU was established at al-Azhar University and at Cairo University "to avoid corruption and security infringements against the ordinary student union election process. This was mired with security interventions and NDP hegemony." However, "when the attempt for electing the parallel student union election was done, the university security and administration attacked the student housing, mainly where the Muslim Brotherhood were living and randomly imprisoned students under the false accusation that the Muslim Brothers were organizing a militia on campus."[70] In 2013 there were other attempts at establishing a parallel SU in private universities, after electoral fraud of the SUs therein. In a private university, for instance, a parallel SU election took place, in which 2,082 students participated, compared to the 200 students who participated in the formal SU elections.

It is evident that these regime policies have had a negative impact on young activists thus far. This impact is not only demobilizing activists, but also having an emotional, economic, and organizational toll against activists. Young activists are anxious and afraid of the state security apparatus and of society at large. The short-term consequence of the increasing repression and co-optation today is movement fragmentation. For instance, a direct consequence of that is the fact that, while many activists are imprisoned, members of their previous networks and organizations are unable to mobilize for their release. The feelings that this create have a double-edged sword: they can lead to political abstention, but they can also lead to radicalization. As previous research has found out, the impact of repression depends on the effectiveness it develops on people's fear. However, "an increase in the severity of repression can arouse not only feelings of fear but also anger," which can become the basis for more mobilization when political opportunities arise.[71]

The regime's strategies and young people's adaptation to these strategies should also be understood within the current stage of the global neoliberal process. The international community's obsession with stability to enhance open markets, and combating south-north migration, along with the increasing discourse of youth securitization are important for understanding why the regime is able to crack down on young activists. The al-Sisi regime has developed a discourse that demonstrates the importance of political "stability" to reform the market-based economy and to stop migration. Hence, the al-Sisi regime's cracking down on "some" young activists who might challenge the stability of the neoliberal order in Egypt seems to be an acceptable trade-off to many international policy makers.[72]

What Is Reform and Change for Young Activists?

Even though the regime perceives young political activists as a threat to the nation, it was clear that the young activists in our sample believed in reforming the system, not revolutionizing it. Their ideas of change were more in line with what Asef Bayat identified as "refolutionary" not "revolutionary" change.[73] Young activists' understanding of and belief in political reform and change were an amalgam of reformist change, shaped by the nature of the neoliberal autocratic system in which they lived, while their demands of freedom, social justice, and change were broad and loosely defined. When Mubarak was ousted from office in February 2011, young activists called on the SCAF and its followers to reform the Mubarak regime's institutions, in particular the Ministry of the Interior, the judiciary, and the army. In addition, they mobilized for modifying the constitution, holding elections, guaranteeing more freedoms for political parties, and enabling a democratization process. However, while their demands were noble, these young activists lacked the imagination or initiative to rule, and they wanted someone else to do it for them.[74]

Young political activists believed that the regime should provide the youth with economic, social, and political rights so that they could live dignified lives. "The least I would expect is to have the minimal number of human rights and dignity, not people being tortured. I wish I could do something, but I can't do anything, because I am afraid," one young woman said.[75] A young member of a political party explained, "I want Egypt to be a state based on institutions, not persons. A state that respects the rule of law, a state which protects human dignity."[76] Meanwhile, a protest-movement participant believed that "change will not happen from below, there has to be a political will from above." This young man argued that "the regime provides the Ministry of Interior and Ministry of Defense with too much money, while the budget allocated to health and education is very low, and without an active policy for changing this, there is no hope for change and development."[77] Another respondent stated that "we need to change the elite and the politics, and then think of how to change society from below. . . . We as a society are a reflection of our political elite."[78]

The most urgent reform in Egypt, according to still another activist, has to be the dismantling of the Ministry of the Interior, stopping torture, and granting freedom of expression to everyone. He added:

> All necessary measures should be taken to end corruption so that Egypt will be developed. Another problem is that we also need to change citizens' perceptions on certain human rights. We live in a society that is in favor of the death sentence, so we need to change society's perception of certain rights as well. . . . The laws and social traditions should be changed; we need more freedoms.[79]

Other activists were convinced that reform and change should come from below. A member of a public university SU argued that for reform to take place, she had to work with the regime instead of in opposition to it. "In the student union we always used to be in the opposition, but we should have entered the union from a reformist perspective. Participation is like unemployment; it depends on the youth themselves."[80] A protest-movement member felt that public awareness should be raised concerning their human rights: "I am trying to teach people their human rights, but I am not appreciated."[81]

Other activists believed that change could be incremental and assisted by applying some international pressure on the regime. One young man in a human rights organization commented that "it is very hard for activists today to be present in the public sphere; however, we can still make some small changes. We were able to get the regime to take out 100 imprisoned activists, because we had a successful international campaign."[82] These ideas of reform and change are also related to young people's positioning within both the global neoliberal system and the current stage of Egypt's securitized, neoliberal system. Young activists' desire for political and social change based on freedom and human rights does not go beyond the ideas of the reformist global system of youth empowerment and democracy promotion. The absence of an imagination to overhaul the system or to abolish social inequalities reflects the impact of the global neoliberal discourses on young "refolutionary" people.

Conclusion

This chapter examined the extent to which the al-Sisi regime perceives young political activists as a threat to the nation, and it also discussed young people's responses to this. The ability of young political activists to mobilize large numbers of citizens against the regime during protest events like the January 25 uprising against Mubarak, the June 2013 demonstrations against Morsi, and later the sit-in at Rab'a Square pushed the regime into strategies of repression, co-optation, and delegitimation by the media. These strategies were effective in frightening activist youth away from political engagement. Many young people have voiced their concern and fear of the regime. They were afraid to mobilize citizens on the streets or even to discuss politics in cafés. An important finding was that young activists also feel intimidated by society at large. The influence of the al-Sisi regime over the media and the media's ability to turn citizens against young activists were shown to be important in deterring young people from political engagement and protests. Young activists expressed their discomfort with the willingness of their fellow citizens to report them to the police. As the result of an ongoing media campaign against youth activists, it is likely that citizen reporting against other citizens, especially young political activists, will increase.[83] The limited venues of participation that are available in today's Egypt for young people who represent the hope are not available for young people who are perceived to be a threat.

Ironically, although the regime perceives these young activists as a threat, they are mostly reformists at heart. They themselves do not perceive themselves or their ideas as a threat to the country, but rather as hope for a better future. Although they "voice" their discontent with the governing elite, they do not call for a complete overturning of the system. In the thirty-three semistructured interviews and five focus groups of this research project, only one young activist believed that the only possible way to develop Egypt was through a revolution, with a complete change of institutions and the ruling elite.[84] The rest of the sample favored incremental reform of the sociopolitical and economic system.

This chapter and the previous one analyzed young people who were civically and politically engaged. Chapter 3 focused mainly on those who were engaged through "tolerable" venues, especially NGOs and tolerated opposition political parties, while the present chapter discussed young people who were engaged in the "intolerable" venues, mainly human rights organizations, certain political parties, and protest movements. The young civically and politically engaged people in both groups are mainly from middle-income families and have university educations. The next chapter sheds light on the marginalized, or young people from low-income family backgrounds. These subaltern classes are generally forgotten and excluded from public policies and debates, and they usually choose to "exit" the political and civic engagement spheres altogether.

5

Youth Poverty

The Marginalized

The number and scope of subaltern groups in public spaces after the January 25 uprising increased dramatically. Street merchants, food-cart vendors, car parkers, and street occupiers grew exponentially across urban Cairo.[1] These developments led to more police and military-led violence. In response, labor demonstrations and strikes have been effectively banned since 2013. The regime actively repressed labor protests and strikes, and it is estimated that hundreds of labor activists and union leaders have been fired during the al-Sisi presidency.[2] Whenever demonstrations took place, police violence intensified, ramping up control over urban space, especially in major cities with more barbed-wire checkpoints, more barricades, and the installation of entrance gates to some downtown Cairo streets.[3] While these security measures were frequently applied against the presence of subaltern groups in the urban public sphere, the regime's fundamental responsibility to provide access to clean water, to healthcare, or even to personal security has decreased.[4]

Who are these subaltern groups—the marginalized young people— and what is the impact of the securitized, neoliberal system on their life chances? Is educational background the main source for enhancing young people's life chances? Here I question the globalized neoliberal discourse about the importance of education for empowerment. I demonstrate that marginalized young people have few chances of attaining higher education levels. Relatedly, if they do receive high education levels, they are the least likely to have good employment opportunities. This chapter further discusses youth precarities and how these are further exacerbated by the current stage of economic development and securitization. The previous chapters discussed the impact of the securitized, neoliberal system on civically and politically engaged young people. In this chapter, I am more concerned with those who are not engaged, through analyzing the survey results. Despite this focus on the survey, I provide some insights from a few young people in the sample who are from low-income family backgrounds.

What Is Marginalization?

Marginalization refers to "a deliberate social construction by the dominant class to achieve specific desirable outcomes of political control, social exclusion and economic exploitation."[5] Being marginal in this case is a social, economic, political, physical, and environmental process and condition under which certain people within a certain polity are subjected.[6] We can identify the marginalized with Guy Standing's analysis of the precariat class.[7] Though Standing discusses the precariat as a "class-in-the-making" in Europe, in the case of Egypt, young marginalized people are conscious about their own deprivations.[8] However, they do not have a common identity beyond that of the nationalized construct of being an Egyptian citizen/commoner/precariat. Hence, I do not discuss the precariat as a separate class; it is rather a continuation of the working class. I use a broader understanding of the working class, which encompasses industrial workers, agricultural workers, and service-sector workers. In addition there are the unemployed and those who work in the informal sector and have irregular incomes. This latter class has different relations of production and distribution and different relations to the state.[9] Analyzing youth from this precariat perspective is important, because understanding social inequalities and changing precariat relations can first be discerned in the youth phase, when young people from different socioeconomic backgrounds first make their transitions to adulthood, and where these changes have implications on the wider state-society relations in the long run.[10]

Marginalization is often perceived as a consequence of poverty. Young people from informal urban areas saw that they were marginalized because of their poverty. One of our respondents living in the informal housing area in Cairo, who worked at a local nongovernmental organization (NGO), explained that this informal settlement is totally

> forgotten by the state. Injustice prevails in informal settlements. There is not one single police station in this whole area and not one single hospital, although according to the last census this informal area is host to 70,000 individuals. Lastly one of my friends saw a big fight on the street where gunshots were exchanged. My friend tried calling the police more than five times, however, with no answer. Even the ambulances do not enter our area.[11]

Young people from low-income families are marginalized by the regime from accessing basic infrastructure and welfare provisions. Nevertheless, repression against them has increased, especially when they call for their basic social and economic rights. The rise of poverty, especially urban poverty, has simultaneously brought repressive measures against the poor and the working classes. According to Saloua Ismail's account of the eighteen-day uprising, the burning down of ninety-nine police stations across Egypt expressed the growing discontent among citizens, especially those residing in the poor, densely populated areas of informal urban settlements (*awsha'iyyat*). "The police stations were sites of violent government through torture, verbal abuse and humiliation, while police officers have long served as agents of everyday government in popular quarters."[12] Subaltern youth (or "harafish," defined by Mohamed Gamal Bashir, a former member of the Ultras White Knights, as "youth with no prospects who often skirt the edge of the law") have burned police stations in their neighborhoods in response to the decades of police oppression against the poor.[13] Security control dramatically increased after the January 25 uprising, with a surge in police attacks against the subaltern poor. In March 2011, when the Supreme Council of the Armed Forces (SCAF) took power, demonstrations and strikes were banned because they disrupted production.[14] Police brutality has been notably apparent in the informal settlements, especially during times of demolitions or evictions. In order to carry these out, the police threaten to arrest, and indeed do arrest, people or even threaten to kill those who try to oppose them. When relocations are ordered, these are done without consultation with the residents.[15]

Even though these young people are already marginalized, and have generally chosen to "exit" the polity, to work in the informal economy, and to live in informal settlements, they sometimes, when time and space permits, have chosen to "voice" their discontent through demonstrations and contestations.

Economic Development and the Rise of Poverty

Economic development indicators were positive for Egypt in the few years prior to the January 25, 2011, uprising, especially in 2010, when GDP growth stood at 5.1 percent compared to 1 percent in 1990. In the immediate aftermath of the uprising, GDP growth receded and fell to 4.3 percent by 2016 (table 5.1). The growth, however, was not reflected in citizens' standards of living or in higher employment levels, particularly among young people, whose unemployment rate rose from 26.3 percent in 1991 to 34.6 percent in 2016 (table 5.1). More importantly, the increase in GDP led to high inflation and lower wages. The weekly earnings per worker in the public sector declined from 542 Egyptian pounds (EGP) in 2010 to EGP465 in 2016.

Paradoxically, the private sector, which is encouraged by various international financial institutions to provide more employment opportunities, offers lower salaries than the public sector, where the mean worker earnings per week dropped from EGP299 in 2010 to EGP270 in 2016.[16] These earnings are below the poverty benchmark of US$5.50 per day specified by the World Bank. While real earnings in both private

TABLE 5.1 Economic Indicators

	1991	2000	2010	2016
GDP per capita (% annual growth)	−1.22	3.43	3.09	2.2
GDP annual growth (%)	1.07	5.36	5.14	4.29
Annual inflation, GDP deflator (%)	18.4	4.94	10.1	6.2
Expenditure on education, total (% of GDP)	4.096*	4.096*	3.76*	N/A
Literacy rate of people 15 and above (%)	44.42*	71.4*	72.04	75.04*
Youth unemployment (ILO estimate, %)	26.3	24.9	28.7	34.6
Poverty headcount ratio at $5.50 a day (% of population)	77.1*	68.1*	72.5	61.9*
Poverty headcount ratio at national poverty lines (% of population)	NA	16.7*	25.2	27.8*

Note: Figures marked with asterisks indicate that data were not available for the year specified; instead, substitutes from the closest year have been included.
Source: World Bank Data, Egypt, online at https://data.worldbank.org/country/egypt-arab-rep.

and public sectors have been decreasing, inflation rates have been on the rise. In June 2011 inflation was 12.1 percent, while by June 2017 it had soared to 33 percent. The consequence of these economic processes has been to negatively impact citizens' lives, with poverty rising from 16.7 percent in 1999 to almost 27.8 percent in 2015 (table 5.1). Thus, the economic growth levels should be taken with a grain of salt, since GDP growth, for example, has added to the volatility and precarity of marginalized young people.

Poverty here is not only a material aspect based on need, or different patterns of deprivation and limited resources, which define poverty as the lack of material goods, like income, wealth, and resources for the accumulation of goods. Another definition of poverty is based on an individual's economic circumstances in general. Here poverty is based on low-income levels, but it is also "the inability to attain the minimum standard of living" in addition to a person's disadvantage in relation to others' economic position in society.[17] Social circumstances are also vital for understanding poverty, where social class, an individual's dependency, lack of security, and exclusion add to their poverty. Thus, poverty not only is about low income, but also encompasses an individual's dependence on aid, his or her low socioeconomic status, vulnerability to various social risks, and lack of basic human rights in addition to being excluded from "participation in the normal pattern of social life."[18]

Economic and Social Marginalization

Egypt offers limited chances for social mobility, according to Harry Pettit, since young people from poor families have few social connections, networking capabilities, or capital.[19] Field research with young people also suggests they believe that if they do not have social connections that can help them to find employment, they will not be able to find it. The increased scarcity in employment opportunities adds to political volatility in developing countries.[20]

The majority of marginalized young people are those whose family income levels are poor, who live in Upper and Lower Egypt, and who have low levels of education, typically less than basic or preparatory education. They are not necessarily unemployed; on the contrary, they are employed but with extreme precariat conditions, and their chance of moving up the social ladder is low due to the cycle of poverty under which they live. In addition, these young people are the least likely to have access to social welfare programs. In the meanwhile, they are "ignored" by the regime. Yet they are the most obedient to the regime, the least likely to mobilize, and are the ones to mostly believe that voting for incumbents during election years is a "duty."

During the qualitative fieldwork, the socioeconomic background of youth was clearly an important issue for young people. The way in which they perceived their role in the polity was indicative of their own socioeconomic background. For instance, young people who had been able to establish small business initiatives or new NGOs were most likely to be from higher economic and educational backgrounds than the rank-and-file members of civil society organizations. Two interviewees asserted that they did not face any obstacles in developing their business organizations; on the contrary, the government supported them. One young man who founded a new NGO to help start-up businesses stated that "if young people want to be included, they can. Everything depends on us." He had been invited to an economic conference in Sharm-el-Sheikh, hosted by al-Sisi, to discuss his start-up initiative.[21] This perception was endorsed by a young woman who grew up in the United States and returned to Egypt as a young faculty member at a private university, who said that she had the power to influence her society positively: "I am not excluded or marginalized at all. I have a lot of privileges like money, social status, social networks, and a family background that does not permit me to be excluded."[22] Another young woman who co-established an NGO for the enhancement of education stated, "I do not see myself as a victim and am therefore not marginalized."[23]

In contrast, young people who were active in civil society organizations and had no tertiary education discussed how marginalized they felt because they came from poor family backgrounds. One young man said that he enjoyed sport, but because he could not afford to join a sports club and did not belong to the mainstream political elite, he was denied the right to participate in a youth center in the Giza governorate.[24] Similarly, young people residing in Upper Egypt and in informal settlements faced the most severe economic and social problems and felt the most marginalized. Within this sample, we had five young people whose experiences confirmed this—four who worked in civil society organizations and one young man who was a member of a political movement. This young man said, "We feel like we do not have any ownership to anything. This is the general feeling for everyone who does not have money in this country."[25] A young woman who lived in a village in Upper Egypt commented that "Egypt is a centralized country, which only provides opportunities to young people in large cities. People in Cairo have many more opportunities than in Upper Egypt."[26] She further argued that, looking at her village, she did not see any change or empowerment either before or after the January 25 uprising.

A young man who was on a scholarship at a private university in Cairo argued that he felt marginalized because his family was from a poorer socioeconomic background than those of his peers.[27] "Exclusion and marginalization are class-based: poor people do not have any voice, middle-class citizens are more or less heard, and upper-class citizens are the most heard in this country."[28] A young activist in a protest movement, who lived in Cairo and worked at a bank, but had a relatively low income, maintained that "we as young people from the lower middle classes and poor classes do not exist for the state. Only those who are sons of intellectuals or elites like judges or lawyers are important and pampered by the state."[29]

Marginalization of these young people was also experienced in their limited access to basic services, especially to healthcare and security. All five young people argued that they were less privileged in their right to access healthcare, for instance. A young man explained that his neighbor had once called an ambulance for a family emergency, but the ambulance driver told him that they could not drive to that informal area. When he had moved the sick person to another street, the ambulance was able to pick her up.[30] A young woman said that "the state does not care about people like us."[31]

These perceptions demonstrate the many social inequalities that occur as a result of the developmentalist and securitized system in Egypt. The production and reproduction of wealth and poverty can be seen in urban spaces across Egypt.[32] These inequalities are spatially based, where the center receives the most attention from the regime. The development of the "modern" city favors the upper middle classes, and it influences the poor negatively.[33] They also exemplify the precarities that prevail when a regime decides to cut all its welfare provisions while, at the same time, it threatens to repress those who might demonstrate against such cuts. Even though young people's perceptions and beliefs in the previous section are not a manifestation of a precariat class consciousness, they show that these resentments can turn into "voice," or contention, once a political opportunity erupts. Young people's increasing informality in the economy, for instance, has had an impact on various historical political crises. When the informal economy fulfills the role of the state in providing citizens with services like education and employment, it means that the regime cannot have bargaining power over these same people.[34]

Education and Empowerment for All?

The highest level of school dropout was found among young people from low-income families. Furthermore, those who reside in Upper and Lower Egypt have fewer chances of higher levels of education, irrespective of their gender. For instance, 26 percent of young people who live in families with below-average incomes had a college or university degree, compared to 40 percent of young people whose family income levels were above average (see table 5.2). In addition, the findings from the fieldwork demonstrate the relationship between a family's income level, education, and young people's life chances. The life experiences of young people vary first and foremost according to their educational level, and then according to their families' income levels. Hence, if a young person has the opportunity to attain a better educational level, his or her chances for a higher standard of living are likely to increase. However, education and employment are connected to a young person's family background. If a young person comes from a poor, disenfranchised family, their chances of completing higher education are slight. The effect of the privatization of public services and the government's reduced commitment to intervene in health and education has also had an impact on poor people's ability to finish their primary and secondary levels of education. The most disenfranchised youth are those who left school prematurely, a large majority of whom are young women. Poverty is the main reason for leaving school at an early age. Consequently, many young men enter the labor market relatively young and earn low salaries, while young women stay at home, marry young, and reproduce the poverty cycle.

TABLE 5.2 Educational Attainment of Young People

	Incomplete elementary	Elementary	Preparatory	Secondary	College	University	Total	N
Total	6	11	11	41	13	18	100	757
Region								
Urban governorates	6	9	7	28	6	44	100	129
Lower Egypt	7	12	11	41	14	15	100	387
Upper Egypt	4	11	13	45	15	11	100	241
Gender								
Male	6	10	10	41	13	19	100	348
Female	6	12	12	41	12	17	100	409
Economic situation of household by national standards								
Above average	3	9	7	41	4	36	100	38
Average	4	10	10	43	12	21	100	451
Below average	10	14	13	37	16	10	100	268
Employment status past 12 months								
Employed	6	12	10	36	13	23	100	322
Not employed	6	10	12	45	12	14	100	435

This table displays characteristics for all youth not currently enrolled in school as of 2016.

On the other hand, young people who have higher educational levels mostly have middle-income family backgrounds and live in major urban cities. Young people from poor backgrounds who live in Upper and Lower Egypt have fewer chances of receiving higher levels of education. Other research has also confirmed this finding. An analysis of the 2010–2011 household survey in Egypt found that young people belonging to the highest 20 percent quintile of society have twice as many chances of attaining a university degree than those in the lowest 20 percent quintile.[35]

Education and Employment Opportunities

Recent reports have shown that the highest unemployment rate in Egypt is among urban educated youth. In 2016 35.8 percent of young people with higher education levels were unemployed and 12.7 percent of young people had an education that was below primary education.[36] Young women have even higher unemployment rates than young men. The main assumption in the literature about young people's problems in the region and in Egypt in particular concerns the relation between education and employment.[37] It is further argued that young educated people are the ones with highest aspirations for employment abroad.[38] Another problem is the fact that the quality of education is poor, and the outcome of education does not support critical thinking.[39] Here, this supposition will be analyzed to bring about a larger picture of what youth marginalization is and who these marginalized youth are.

The survey for the Power2Youth research project was carried out in eight governorates of Egypt between April 17 and May 10, 2016 (for details, see chapter 3). At the time of the interviews, 31 percent of respondents were still enrolled in an educational institution (11 percent in a secondary school, 3 percent in college, and 17 percent at a university). Among those who had ended their education, 17 percent had left before completing basic schooling, 11 percent had basic education, 41 percent had secondary education, 13 percent had achieved a college degree, and 18 percent had attained university education (table 5.2).[40]

The survey showed that 33 percent of young people were employed during the previous twelve months. Among those who did not work in the reference period, 42 percent were students, while 36 percent were either housewives or engaged in domestic tasks (table 5.3). Of those who were employed, 23 percent worked in the private sector, 3 percent worked on a farm that was owned or rented by their households, 5 percent worked in private businesses, and 2 percent worked in the public sector. If we take out the 42 percent of students and 36 percent of

TABLE 5.3 Employment Status in 2016

	Employed	Not employed	Total	
				N
Total	33	67	100	1,200
Region				
Urban governorates	36	64	100	210
Lower Egypt	36	64	100	592
Upper Egypt	28	72	100	398
Gender				
Male	59	41	100	560
Female	8	92	100	634
Postsecondary	53	47	100	241
Economic situation of household by national standards				
Above average	27	73	100	97
Average	32	68	100	711
Below average	38	62	100	392

housewives, we find that 16 percent either had not found a job or had not found an appropriate job. Of these 16 percent, the majority are young people who had university-level education; 46 percent of these had university degrees, compared to 8 percent of those with less than basic education. These findings confirmed previous findings in the region, all of which argue that the highest unemployment levels are among the highly educated in the region.[41]

Young people in cities from low-income families with high education are also less likely to be employed than their peers with high education and middle to higher income levels.[42] Even though these young people attend the same public universities as the middle-income young people, they lack the social networks that could provide them with access to good jobs with decent salaries.[43]

The survey further confirmed that employment opportunities were linked to a young person's networks and the ability of close and extended family to help find them work. Seventy-six percent of employed young people found their jobs either through relatives (47 percent) or friends (29 percent). Only 17 percent of employed youth were the main bread-winners in their families. Qualitative fieldwork has shown the same trends, with some young people reporting that they work in jobs that are not compatible with their educational qualifications, because they did not have connections with people who could help find them work in their fields of interest. One young man who worked as an administra-tor in a development organization explained, "I couldn't find a proper job based on my educational background. I also wanted to work at a well-known civil society organization. However, it is hard to find a place there, because it is known that youth who work in [these] large organi-zations have to have connections."[44] Another young man said that "so many jobs are closed off against young people from poor backgrounds. The public sector only allows certain connected people to their jobs. . . . I searched for a job for a very long time, [and] even though I have a business degree, I work in another field today."[45] A young woman living in an informal settlement, who received a bachelor's degree in political science in 2012 from the public university, told a similar story:

> I tried to find a job in the public sector. First I tried in different minis-tries, but after many attempts, I never received an answer. I believe this is because I do not have "wasta" [cronyism or nepotism-based connec-tions]. Now I am working at the local NGO here, it is a decent job, and I am helping children from my community have better education and better chances, but this is not what I initially thought or wanted to do with my life.[46]

This confirmed the view that young people who network themselves or have family or friends that can help them through "wasta" stood a much higher chance of finding employment than their peers with the same educational attainment but from poorer families. This also cor-responds with the perception among young people of the importance of wasta for getting a job. For instance, when asked about this, 81 percent of young men and 69 percent of young women believed that wasta was important. In addition, 77 percent and 74 percent of young people with average and below-average income levels agreed with this. Furthermore, the majority of young people interviewed during the qualitative field-work argued that if a young person did not have wasta, it was unlikely (or near impossible) that he or she would find a job or receive a decent salary. One young man said that "it is humiliating for young people who have master's degrees and PhDs to [have to] demonstrate to demand an increase to EGP1,000 per month . . . while on the other hand, someone who has worse education, but has wasta, finds a better paying job. . . . This is very problematic."[47]

Young people's perception of their own unemployment or underem-ployment shows that the basic source of resentment is corruption and cronyism.[48] Hence, for young people, the problem is less the scarcity of employment opportunities and more bad governance. They do not question the realities of the market economy or the ability of the public or private sectors to create employment opportunities. They also believe that education is capable of empowering young people. However, the root cause of their own unemployment or underemployment is beyond these macro structures. According to recent figures from Transparency International's corruption perception index, Egypt's score is 35 out of 100 in 2019, below the international average of 43.[49] Thus young people's perceptions of corruption and cronyism being the main impediment for their own well-being have statistical validity.

Youth Precarities

According to Guy Standing, the precariat is rarely paid for holidays, medical leaves, or any welfare entitlements from the state. One of the important aspects of being precariat is having to live under various uncertainties.[50] In the case of the Middle East and Egypt, these precar-ities are even more accentuated, provided the fact that young people have to endure this precariousness under an increasingly securitized and repressive regime.

The employment conditions are rather uncertain, with only 18 percent of those who are employed having access to health insurance. It is important and ironic to note that only 1 percent of young people with less than basic education (that is, the poor and marginalized) and only 1 percent of the highly educated young people have access to health insurance. On the other hand, 61 percent of young people of middle-class or working-class backgrounds have insurance. This can be traced back to the fact that they might be working as laborers in factories, which are bound to provide health insurance by law. These are most likely to be young people who work for wage salaries in the public and private sectors.

Only 20 percent of the employed young people had work contracts, and the difference between educational levels is stark: only 1 percent for young people with less than basic education have contracts compared to 45 percent of university educated. There were no employment benefits for 75 percent of young people who were employed; even sick leave is only granted to 16 percent of those who are employed. The difference between those who are educated and those who are not is also stark in this case. For those who had less than basic education, 89 percent had no access to any benefits at all, 2 percent received paid sick leave, and 5 percent free meals. This is compared to 49 percent of people with university education who said they do not have access to any benefits.

Temporary employment is among 41 percent of the employed young, while 9 percent have seasonal employment and only 29 percent have permanent jobs. The highest percentage of permanent job holders are among the university educated at 39 percent. When asked how often they work in physically unpleasant conditions, 68 percent said that they are either often, sometimes, or always subjected to physically unpleasant conditions. The highest percentages again are among the lowest educated, with 80 percent compared to 58 percent of the highly educated. Young people's fear of losing their jobs is also high. Seventy-two percent said that they fear losing their jobs a lot or a little. The average monthly income for young people with secondary-school diplomas or university degrees was between EGP1,000–2,999 in 2016.[51] The difference is stark here, with 67 percent of university educated having this average compared to 46 percent of those with less than basic education. Not surprisingly, 59 percent are dissatisfied with their earnings. The majority of young people, 76 percent, are dissatisfied with the government's efforts to secure employment for youth. Education levels do not make a difference in this matter.

These precarities are related to the past two decades' economic reforms, which have gone hand in hand with the global neoliberal project. Many of the existing precarities are a result of neoliberal economic developments, proposed by various Egyptian economists. According to Angela Joya, liberal think tanks in Egypt have blamed youth unemployment on "labour market rigidities—such as minimum wage legislation, employment protection, working time regulations, overtime pay, trade unions and social security contributions."[52] From this perspective, if these workers' rights are abolished, the private sector and international corporations would have more incentives to hire young people. Relatedly, reforms on workers' rights to strike have also been implemented, where striking has become illegal.[53] Thus these so-called market reforms have increased youth precarities, poverty, and marginalization. Hence, poverty and marginalization here are a result of how these young people are incorporated into the market economy, rather than their exclusion from the market.[54] This has been developing hand in hand with the expansion of the informal sectors, where there are virtually no contracts.[55] Young people themselves also perceive the private sector negatively. One young man argued that "the private sector is dysfunctional. If a university graduate finds a job, it is for a very bad salary, and there is no room for negotiation: you either have to take it or leave it."[56] This partially explains why young people are interested in working for the public sector and also why those who are unemployed, especially young women and students, choose not to work outside their households.

These precariat conditions are also a regional phenomenon. It is believed that the expansion of the private sector, especially the service sector, was tied to changes in employment patterns that were becoming more insecure.[57] The Central Agency for Public Mobilization and Statistics recently reported that the average weekly income in the public sector is higher than that of the private sector. It also demonstrates that women have better income levels in the public sector than in the private sector.[58]

Marginalization and Nonparticipation

The literature on youth civic and political participation in the region demonstrates that middle-class and highly educated individuals tend to be the most active participants in civil society organizations and in voting in elections. This was also discussed extensively in the previous two chapters.[59] Voting behavior is also analyzed extensively in the region, as many scholars demonstrate that the poor tend to vote in order to receive perks.[60] This part of my research moves beyond the literature to analyze the tendency to vote for receiving perks, instead I discuss the extent to which the poor participate in elections compared to the rest of the population.

As shown in the previous two chapters, only 3 percent of young people participate in civil society organizations. Of young people in Lower and Upper Egypt, those who have the lowest levels of education, and those who belong to low-income family backgrounds and those who are unemployed, are the least likely to be members of civil society. The pattern is also similar when it comes to understanding which young people tend to try to develop small groups to solve problems within their communities. These are 7 percent of young people according to the survey. Young people from Upper and Lower Egypt with the least educational backgrounds, with below-average income levels, and who are unemployed tend to be the least likely to participate.[61]

TABLE 5.4 Membership in an Organization

	Model	Model 2
Unemployed	−0.03*	−0.03*
	(0.01)	(0.01)
Lower household income	−0.01	
	(0.01)	
Higher education	0.00	
	(0.02)	
Incomplete primary education	−0.04***	−0.04***
	(0.01)	(0.01)
Adj. R-squared	0.02	0.02

Standard errors in parentheses.
$*p < .05; **p < .01; ***p < .001.$

To further understand the extent to which the poor youth are marginalized from participation in organizations, I constructed an ordinary least-squares (OLS) model where membership in civil society organizations is the dependent variable, while the independent variables are unemployment, low household income levels, high education levels, and incomplete primary-education levels. It is clear from table 5.4 that education plays a significant role, where those young people who have less than a basic education are least likely to participate in civil society organizations.

Voting in parliamentary elections has higher percentages of participation in general, with 47 percent of young people having voted in the 2015 parliamentary elections. Even though young people with better education standards and higher family-income levels are more likely to have participated in these elections, the least educated have participated at 39 percent and 23 percent, respectively. In contrast, those with below-average income levels have tended to participate at a higher percentage (49 percent) than those with an average income level. When asked why they voted, 44 percent of respondents said it was a duty and 36 percent said that they wanted change. Of these, there is a stark difference between the educated compared to the less educated (table 5.5). For

TABLE 5.5 Answers to "Why Did You Participate in These Parliamentary Elections?"

	"Duty"	"Support incumbents"	"Want change"	"Pressure from family/ friends"	Other	Total	
							N
Total	44	10	36	9	1	100	541
Region							
Urban governorates	42	6	47	6	—	100	96
Lower Egypt	47	11	34	7		100	277
Upper Egypt	40	13	33	12	2	100	168
Gender							
Male	40	12	41	5	1	100	290
Female	49	8	29	13		100	251
Highest education completed							
Less than basic	57	11	16	16	—	100	81
Preparatory/ Basic	52	12	19	11	6	100	50
Secondary	43	10	39	8	1	100	250
Postsecondary	37	11	46	6	—	100	160
Economic situation of household by national standards							
Above average	38	7	51	3	1	100	51
Average	48	11	34	7		100	314
Below average	38	11	36	13	1	100	176
Employment status for past twelve months							
Employed	44	14	35	6	1	100	210
Not employed	44	7	37	11		100	331

instance, 57 percent of young people who did not finish their primary education said that it was a duty, compared to 37 percent of those with a university education. Those who are interested in voting for change also portray the same patterns where only 16 percent of the least educated have voted for change, while 46 percent of the highest educated have voted for change.[62] The survey questions did not ask whether voters received perks form different incumbents or not, and our qualitative fieldwork did not ask this either.

In order to test for the likelihood of young people from poor backgrounds voting and aiming to discern whether young voters receive perks or not, I constructed another OLS model, where the dependent variable is voting in the last parliamentary elections, while the independent variables are unemployment, lower household-income levels, high education levels, and incomplete primary-education levels. The analysis in table 5.5 demonstrates that young people with less than a primary education are the least likely to vote, where there is a negative correlation with elections. Meanwhile, those who have high education levels are more likely to vote. Hence, vote buying might be important in some districts, or among some poor people as argued in a previous work on vote buying in Egypt, yet, in general, a low education level is an indicator of marginalization and less voting.

Even though online activism is not an indicator of protest activities in general, for the purposes of this chapter, I use it as an indicator for such, since other questions on activism were not allowed in the questionnaire.[63] Interestingly, the results in table 5.6 demonstrate that unemployed young people and young people with low education levels are not likely to be online activists. Similar to voting and membership in civil society organizations, online activism is negatively associated with young people who have low education levels.

Studies on political participation and mobilization of the poor in other developing regions of the world have also found similar results. For instance, a large-N study on the relation between poverty and participation found that poverty decreases civic and political participation

TABLE 5.6 Vote in Last Parliamentary Elections

	Model 1	Model 2
Unemployed	0.11	
	(0.05)	
Lower household income	−0.02	
	(0.04)	
High education	0.13*	0.16***
	(0.05)	(0.04)
Incomplete primary education	−0.23***	−0.22***
	(0.04)	(0.03)
Adj. R-squared	0.09	0.08

Standard errors in parentheses.
$*p < 0.10, **p < 0.05, ***p < 0.01.$

TABLE 5.7 Online Activism

	Model 1	Model 2
Unemployed	−0.12***	−0.13***
	(0.04)	(0.05)
Lower household income	−0.04	
	(0.03)	
High education	0.10**	0.11**
	(0.04)	(0.04)
Incomplete primary education	−0.09**	−0.12***
	(0.03)	(0.03)
Adj. R-squared	0.04	0.03

Standard errors in parentheses.
$*p < 0.10, **p < 0.05, ***p < 0.01.$

of individuals in different contexts.[64] In Mexico, for instance, findings indicate that the changing economic structure with the increasing neoliberalization of development have created obstacles and have disincentivized the poor from political mobilization and participation. The cost for political participation through increasing securitization has increased for the poor, and hence they have become more pessimistic about participation. "The net effect of institutional reforms, therefore, has been to stifle poor people's political activity, especially in comparison with more affluent groups."[65]

Nevertheless, as Diane Singerman argues, even though disenfranchised and popular classes are marginalized and ignored by the regime, they still can and do engage through various activities that may sometimes be overlooked. She contends that her research in one subaltern community in Cairo "suggests that excluded communities can develop creative and effective strategies to accomplish shared goals, despite the intentions and policies of political elites and the constraints that their security apparatus places on political participation and freedoms of expression and associations."[66]

Marginalization and Trust

Trust in general, and social trust in particular, is important for various reasons and is desirable in both democratic as well as authoritarian regimes. In democratic regimes, individuals who believe that others in their society can be trusted tend to participate more in politics, have positive views of their democratic procedure, governments, and institutions, and are more active in civic life. Social trust is then related to social capital.[67] Social capital from a liberal perspective refers to the "features of social organization such as trust, norms and networks that can improve the efficiency of society by facilitating coordination action."[68] The more social trust exists within a certain polity, the more likely that this society has social capital attributes. Low trust levels are likely to decrease the development of social capital, which is believed to be important for strengthening democracies.[69] Social trust is also desirable in authoritarian regimes, as it supports the status quo and the legitimacy of the regime in question. Here, trust is related to the performance of a particular regime.[70] Hence, if social trust is low, then the legitimacy of the regime becomes questionable. The relationship between marginalization and social and political trust becomes interesting in this case as it sheds light on the impact of marginality on young people, how they distrust society at large, and how low their social capital is. However, it also demonstrates the fact that, implicitly, the legitimacy of the regime itself is questionable.

The survey revealed that the majority of young people lacked trust in formal institutions, and 61 percent believed that they needed to be careful when dealing with other people. While a high 98 percent expressed complete trust in their immediate families, and 62 percent in their extended families, 23 percent had complete trust in their neighbors, 17 percent complete trust in coworkers, and a small 2 percent trusted people from other nationalities. The trend became more distrustful with formal institutions; only 9 percent of young people had complete confidence in the printed press. The level of confidence in information from TV and the internet was higher at 30 percent for both. Confidence in local government and political parties stood at a mere 2 percent. Confidence in women's organizations and charitable organizations was 10 percent and 47 percent, respectively. Trust levels, unlike other variables, were not determined by educational and income levels; they are attributable to youth in general, rather than to those who are poor or marginalized in particular.

These generally low trust levels show that the neoliberal economy backed by an increasingly securitized regime has had the effect of increasing trust among family networks and friends, but of reducing wider social solidarity and trust. The majority of young people, irrespective of their educational or income level, trust their families and close relatives completely as argued above. These people are the most likely to provide assistance and help youth network with others to find employment. These figures can also be attributed to the increasing levels of informal economy and social networks that function as a result of precariat economic and social conditions and neoliberal developments. The informal networks are developed by young people's families and communities, which facilitate the accumulation of savings among family, friends, and neighbors; they also facilitate employment opportunities and enhanced education in addition to goods and services.[71] These provide support and help for the subaltern groups, which cannot be provided by the regime or by the formal networks within the polity.

On the other hand, trust in other people is low. Seventeen percent and 39 percent trust completely and trust somewhat, respectively, their coworkers. It seems that being marginalized and having less trust in institutions is related to the structure and culture of the neoliberal system at large, rather than to individual human and social capital development per se.[72] Beyond social trust, it is important to reflect on the low political trust levels as indicators of low perceptions of legitimacy toward the regime. In autocracies, high trust levels can serve the regime's legitimacy, while low trust levels demonstrate citizens' skepticism toward that same regime and might indicate loss of legitimacy.[73]

Conclusion

The relationship between the securitized, authoritarian, neoliberal system and marginalization has been highlighted in this chapter through demonstrating the impact of this system on the life chances of subaltern youth. It is evident that this system in which Egyptian young people live has added to youth marginalization.

Since Nasser and Sadat, subsequent regimes have increased access to education; however, quality education has been compromised. In addition, in order to reduce budget deficits and to apply neoliberal policies as required, Egyptian policy makers and leaders have concocted an amalgam of increased security control and reduced social welfare provisions. This has added to the burden of young people and has diminished their opportunities for better life chances. The analysis confirmed that the most marginalized young people were those with no education. They were from low-income family backgrounds, were marginalized in the labor market, earned the lowest incomes, are subjected to the most dangerous physical conditions, and have the fewest work benefits compared to their peers. It has also demonstrated that if a young person is from a poor background and has higher education, their chances of good employment opportunities are dim. This requires further assessment and analysis of the general global discourse that stresses the importance of education for better life chances. Social networks in this regard are more important than education per se. This chapter has also demonstrated the fact that the marginalized young people, like the civically and politically engaged young people, do not want an overhaul of the current neoliberal developmental process. They do not imagine an alternative model for development. They only want good governance and an end to corruption.

A consequence of poverty and marginality is also the low interest in civic and political life. Subaltern young people do not only "exit" the public and political spheres, but they also "exit" the formal employment spheres, through finding jobs in the informal economy. Highly educated youth from a low-income family background were the most likely not to find employment, while others, especially those from richer families, had higher chances for employment. Even though young women theoretically have equal chances for secondary and higher education, their life experiences differed from those of young men, especially regarding employment opportunities. Marginalized young people have largely chosen to exit the system, through living on the margins.

In the next chapter, the dynamics of youth as promise (and hope of the nation or as loyalty) and youth as peril (and threat to the nation) and poor, marginalized youth will be further discussed in the context of the current phase of political transformations in similar regimes in the Middle East and North Africa.

6

Dilemmas of Participation and Nonparticipation in the MENA Region

Young people in the Middle East and North Africa (MENA) region, like their counterparts in Egypt, are an important unit of analysis during this contemporary era of social and political transformation. The region has been characterized by authoritarian regimes that have held onto power for several decades. Their power structures have been threatened by a rising wave of youth protests, culminating in the Arab uprisings of 2011 and later a second wave of uprisings in different Arab countries starting in Morocco in 2017. Today, as in the decade preceding the uprisings, the global discourse has revolved around the dichotomy between the positivity discourse of youth as partners in development and the securitization discourse of young people being a security threat.

Initially the discourse on security threat started with the youth bulge during a period of stalled economic growth, and later as the source of political upheavals, civil wars, terrorism, and emigration to Europe and the United States.[1] Recent developments in the region, especially the commitment to market-oriented economic reforms, have given rise to securitized, authoritarian, neoliberal regimes of sorts that have imposed harsh controls through their security apparatuses. MENA regimes are faced with two "contradictory *logics* of rule: the one cultivating desires for market freedom, upward mobility, and consumer pleasure, and the other tethering advancement opportunities to citizen obedience and coercive regulation."[2] Young people are at the heart of this dilemma. As a social category they make claims that manifest state-society relations. They also articulate the fears of the present in addition to presenting the hopes of the future.[3]

This chapter builds on the political economy of youth approach, to analyze the extent to which young people are structurally positioned within the MENA, specifically in Morocco, Tunisia, Turkey, Lebanon, and the Occupied Palestinian Territories (OPT). What is the impact of the political economy of authoritarianism on young people's life experiences? Why and how do young people engage civically and politically in their respective regimes? In parallel to the Power2Youth (P2Y) research in Egypt, the same quantitative and qualitative analyses took place in Tunisia, Morocco, the OPT, Lebanon, and Turkey from April 2015 until November 2016. The quantitative fieldwork is based on a large-N survey study conducted by the Fafo Research Foundation for the P2Y research project. Between October 2015 and August 2016, almost identical national representative surveys of youth aged eighteen to twenty-nine were carried out in the six Middle Eastern countries under analysis. A total of 7,579 young people participated in the survey in all six countries.[4]

Neoliberalism and the Promotion of Civil Society in the Region

The global neoliberal project has been adopted in one way or the other in almost all the MENA countries.[5] As discussed in chapter 1, neoliberal economic developments became closely tied to patronage and crony capitalism. Patronage and crony capitalism require the restructuring of state institutions, with the state taking over the privatization process, by either passing legislation or introducing mechanisms for opening the market to new business entrants.[6] The privatization process, which was supported by the international financial institutions (IFIs) in the region from the 1990s onward, has been marred by corruption and clientelism, with government officials taking large sums of money to endorse the rush toward privatization.[7] The links between the political and economic elites strengthened and added to the disenfranchisement of the majority of the population.[8] These trends inhibited young people's ability to participate in the various spheres of life.[9] They also led to high poverty levels and high unemployment, and to labor informality, in addition to undercutting the social support mechanisms. Young people have been the most affected by these changes.[10]

> At the same time as governments meted out repression against those who resisted [the] neoliberal turn, the new policies also very much depended upon the cultivation of a domestic social base. A myriad of institutional actors were involved in this process. . . . Their policy choices helped to advance a shift in the structures of the state itself, acting to protect and foster a powerful bourgeoisie that grew in the interstices of the changing economy.[11]

The MENA regimes have tried to lessen the socioeconomic pressures on the middle and lower classes through supporting the development of civil society organizations, especially nongovernmental organizations (NGOs). These NGOs fill the gap of government nonintervention in the market, while at the same time bringing some young people into the sphere of regime influence. In this sense, civil society can help in the social protection provisions, such as access to education and healthcare, which the governments are no longer providing. These organizations have a dual function for these regimes. They develop the welfare that the state is unable to provide, while at the same time they are contained and co-opted by the regimes.[12]

Within this structural containment and neoliberal reforms, young people both affect and are affected by these structures, adding to the trends of social and political continuity and change in the region. These corporate strategies have not always worked to the advantage of the regimes in question, and while neoliberal advancement has helped incorporate a large number of young people to the regimes' side, it has also increased the number and scope of contestations against these same regimes.

This chapter analyzes five MENA regimes, which have different authoritarian arrangements and regime types and that have experienced varying degrees of demonstrations and uprisings, ranging from small-scale protests during the 2011 uprisings in Morocco and the OPT, to large waves of uprisings in Tunisia, and major demonstrations in Turkey and Lebanon a few years after the Arab uprisings. The second wave of demonstrations in the region has also hit some of these same countries, mainly Morocco in 2017 and Lebanon in 2019 and 2020. While this chapter discusses the dynamics of the first wave of demonstrations, there are many commonalities between both the first and second waves. The regimes' strategies toward young people have been similar as the governments in question developed exclusionist and repressive strategies against young people belonging to the opposition, who are perceived as a threat to the nation.

Youth Civic and Political Participation

Within the authoritarian, securitized, neoliberal system in which young people live today, different MENA regimes have supported the development of civil society organizations, and of NGOs in particular, in an attempt to contain young people who are in political opposition to their regimes. Civil society organizations in the case of the MENA region are closely tied to authoritarian regimes; they reproduce the authoritarian system, where the associational context in these regimes is dominated by authoritarian tendencies, and patron-client relations of authorities. These organizations in and of themselves can replicate this system and add to the authoritarian structure.[13] Thus young people who are civically and politically engaged through mainstream civil society organizations and political parties—or those who are perceived as a hope for the nation—can help in sustaining the status quo, yet as in the case of Egypt, these same young people can at certain times of distress "exit" from participation or "voice" their discontent through other means.

The percentage of young people who belong to civil society organizations is not high in the countries under analysis. They range from 5.5 percent membership in organizations, as in Turkey, to 12.2 percent as in Morocco (table 6.1). Civic participation at the local community level

TABLE 6.1 Membership in a Civil Society Organization

	Turkey		Palestine		Tunisia		Lebanon		Morocco	
	Freq.	%	Freq.	%	Freq.	%	Freq.	%	Freq.	%
"Yes"	98	5.48	59	9.77	82	6.88	87	8.7	125	12.23
"No"	1,689	94.52	545	90.23	23	1.93	912	91.2	894	87.48
No answer	0	0	0	0	51	4.28	1	0.1	3	0.3
Total	1,787	100	604	100	1,191	100	1,000	100	1,022	100

TABLE 6.2 Participation in Local Community Activities to Solve Problems

	Turkey		Palestine		Tunisia		Lebanon		Morocco	
	Freq.	%	Freq.	%	Freq.	%	Freq.	%	Freq.	%
"Yes"	158	8.84	179	29.64	117	9.82	168	16.8	293	28.67
"No"	1,627	91.05	423	70.03	1,045	87.74	828	82.8	716	70.06
No answer	2	0.11	2	0.33	29	2.44	4	0.4	13	1.27
Total	1,787	100	604	100	1,191	100	1,000	100	1,022	100

tends to be higher, as young people seem to have more ownership in their own small communities. For instance, participation in local community activity ranged from 8.9 percent in Turkey to 28.7 percent in Morocco (table 6.2).

Young people in the Palestinian Territories were an interesting example where authoritarian adjustments take place. Here, it is not only about the impact of the political economy of authoritarianism on the national level, but here the interaction between the international community, especially the donor community, and young people is at play. Historically, Palestinian youth were associated with the Palestinian national movement to liberate Palestinian territories from Zionist occupation. Nevertheless, after the 1993 Oslo Accords, young people were no longer perceived as an active collective force for decolonization, but rather as individuals who needed to be contained and supported to become active participants and supporters of the then newly established Palestinian Authority (PA).[14] The Ministry of Youth and Sports was set up by the PA, and youth became integrated into the development sector to depoliticize them. International funding agencies have also contributed to the efforts of depoliticization by providing young people with incentives to engage in their own capacity building and individual leadership.[15] Considering the political divide between the West Bank and the Gaza Strip, each political authority, whether it be Hamas in Gaza or the PA in the West Bank, encourages young people to participate within their own political territory. The Higher Council of Youth and Sports based in Ramallah performs the same function as the PA's security services in curtailing the activities of young people who support Hamas in the West Bank, and vice versa.[16] According to a member of an NGO, "In the '80s the young people were involved in the liberation efforts, but now there is no longer one main goal any more. The parties are not interested in change and in youth participating in that."[17]

Palestinian youth have high numbers of civic and political participation compared to youth in the rest of the countries under analysis. Many young Palestinians are part of mainstream civil society organizations and NGOs. Even though they believe that being part of civil society is important, they themselves see their own roles in these organizations as marginal. One of the main problems they envision is the fact that the majority of NGO work is donor-driven, and hence the objectives of the work and civil society are not to enhance and develop Palestinian society per se, but instead to develop what the international community deems best for Palestinians. For instance, one young interviewee argued, "We are kidding ourselves . . . ; once we are gone [the time period is finished and/or the budget spent] the activity immediately stops. There are some projects we care about very much and we try to sustain them even when the funding has ended, but we know that once we are not able to continue following up at [the] location, the activity will stop."[18]

Similarly in Turkey, a large number of civil society actors, in particular NGOs, have come to the fore of development projects. These organizations are funded by different international actors, especially the European Union. Young people observe that these organizations mobilize young people to work on certain developmental issues. However, these issues represent important international projects, not the "needs" of young people or needs for the development of Turkey per se.[19]

Participation in civil society organizations is highest among young people in Morocco (see table 6.1). Yet during qualitative fieldwork with the country's young people, researchers found that respondents do not perceive young Moroccans to be civically and politically engaged. Instead, young people felt marginalized within their own civil society organizations and political parties. One focus-group participant in Rabat, for instance, argued that after entering the party "the young people had different behaviors: First, those who changed their behavior in order to cope with the system. Second, those who became disappointed and then disinterested in politics and left the party. Third, those who chose to fight back but were crushed by the party, marginalized and then joined a disgruntled minority group within the party."[20]

In Lebanon after the civil war, young people became more active in "interest-based" NGOs. These NGOs advocate environmental protection, help people with disabilities, or mobilize for democratic elections.[21] After the assassination of Rafik Hariri in 2005 another wave of NGOs emerged, based mostly in Beirut. They were mainly concerned with humanitarian projects, reconstruction, and peaceful coexistence matters.[22] Nevertheless, these NGOs were soon to disappear in favor of NGOs that were linked to various sectarian denominations. In general, since the end of the Lebanese civil war and the signing of the Ta'if agreement in 1989 the sectarian elite's strategies neutralized Lebanon's civil society actors and depoliticized them. This has been important in sustaining the sectarian status quo in Lebanon ever since.[23] Interestingly, young people working in different NGOs that help in capacity building argue that for sociopolitical and economic change to occur, young people should work within the current sectarian structure to strive for reform from within.[24] Youth participation in political parties and NGOs is perceived positively in Lebanon when it does not threaten the dominant political, social, or moral order of society. Similarly in Morocco, for instance, young people are aware of the linkage between authoritarian resilience and civil society participation, yet they are "optimistic; young people have a role to play and we must unite our voice, develop the role of civil society."[25]

Participation in the political sphere is also promoted by the different regimes. For instance, many young people are members of different political parties through membership in the parties' youth branches. However, according to a large number of young people in these countries, these branches do not influence party policies: they just rubber-stamp the decisions that have already been taken at higher levels in the party leadership.[26]

In Turkey for instance, the Justice and Development Party (AKP) developed a national youth council that mobilized a large number of young people into its ranks. However, many in Turkey believe that this movement of young people into the AKP's youth wing entrenched the AKP's hegemony over the political system.[27] Although young people have often been marginalized from decision-making in their respective organizations or political parties, regimes still perceive them as important strategic partners for the political elite, as well as for the powerful IFIs who believe in the importance of a civil society presence for the entrenchment of the neoliberal process.[28]

Young people belonging to Islamist political parties or movements are interesting cases of young people who are perceived differently based on their regimes. For some regimes like Morocco and Turkey, the youth are mostly co-opted in the political system, while for other regimes like Tunisia they are considered to be a threat to the social order. They are even considered in some countries as "terrorists," as are young members of the Muslim Brotherhood in Egypt and young people in the Salafi movement in Tunisia. In Morocco, the monarchy gained legitimacy through its Islamist heritage and has long tolerated young Islamists, permitted members of Islamist political movements to mobilize, and integrated them into the regime's ranks. The Sufi and the Salafi movements are important in this regard. Sufi movements have been particularly encouraged by the regime in Morocco, since they promote religious tolerance. More recently, they have been attracting young people. The

Salafi movement has also been tolerated during the past decade. King Mohamed VI granted a political pardon to several Salafi leaders who were believed to be linked to the 2003 Casablanca bombings. This created a new pact between the monarch and the Salafists. The Salafists have accepted and supported the king's legitimacy, while he has accepted their integration in moderate Islamist parties such as the Renaissance and Virtue Party.[29]

In Turkey, young people belonging to the Islamist movements, in particular to the ruling AKP, are the most tolerated youth. They receive various perks and are encouraged to participate in both the civic and political spheres.[30] As in the OPT and the European Union, the Euro-Mediterranean Youth Programme that was established in the 1990s was essential in depoliticizing a large number of civically and politically engaged young people.[31] According to one focus-group participant, "The government's activities seek to create a kind of 'ideal youth.' This is through developing youth organizations close to the government. The regime in Turkey wants 'a dutiful child, a soldier and a worker who don't cause problems.'"[32] These young people's perceptions of themselves in the polity represent interesting dynamics, where they believe that reform and change rest on their civic and political engagement through working within the authoritarian structure. Yet they want to have more influence over the decision-making processes, whether in civil society organizations, political parties, or in the political context at large. Their perceptions of change and reform are largely harmonious with their regimes' developmental and political models, yet they want to become part of this process, rather than be marginalized.

Youth Activism

While some young people have chosen to participate through formal means within the accepted norms of civic and political participation, others preferred to participate through other ways, mainly through demonstrations, protest movements, or online activism. Participation through protest movements in the region ranged from 2 percent in Turkey to 11 percent in the OPT (table 6.3). Participation in peaceful demonstrations, however, was much higher, from 5.5 percent in Turkey to almost 17 percent in the OPT (table 6.4). Participation in online activism tended to be lower than in demonstrations, with the only exception being in the OPT (table 6.5). Much of the literature and many of the young people interviewed during the project's fieldwork commended the role of social media in mobilization and in participation, but it was evident that street politics represented more opposition than online. Although social media might be a popular tool for participation, it remains one among others.

As discussed above, young people who are perceived as a threat to the social order are not perceived equally in the MENA regimes under analysis. In Tunisia after Bin Ali's ouster, for instance, the interim government was criticized and two new movements, Kasbah 1 and Kasbah 2, were established to prevent the political elite under Bin Ali from regaining political power.[33] Nevertheless, since these young people were secular, they were more tolerated than the youth from Islamist political backgrounds. Some Salafists who found public-sector employment were forced to cut their beards. "The doors are open to young people who show that they are 'modernists' and to young people who are unveiled. . . . These are included in the civic and political activities. . . . Salafists are more exposed to controls and abuses coming from the security forces."[34]

In Turkey, however, young people from Islamist backgrounds, mainly those belonging to or favoring the ruling AKP party, were the most tolerated in the social and political spheres. Young people in opposition to the AKP rule or in support of Kurdish rights are perceived as a threat. In May 2013, the Gezi Park protesters were interesting examples both of the threat and also of the hope turning to a threat. The Gezi protests were formed by young people from diverse backgrounds. Some were members of protest movements, while others had joined in demonstrations for the first time. According to a field study by Gümüs and Yilmaz,

TABLE 6.3 Participation in Protest Movements

	Turkey		Palestine		Tunisia		Lebanon		Morocco	
	Freq.	%	Freq.	%	Freq.	%	Freq.	%	Freq.	%
"Yes"	37	2.07	68	11.26	117	9.82	51	5.1	41	4.01
"No"	1,748	97.82	530	87.75	1,038	87.15	930	93	965	94.42
No answer	2	0.11	6	0.99	36	3.02	19	1.9	16	1.6
Total	1,787	100	604	100	1,191	100	1,000	100	1,022	100

TABLE 6.4 Attendance at Peaceful Demonstrations

	Turkey		Palestine		Tunisia		Lebanon		Morocco	
	Freq.	%	Freq.	%	Freq.	%	Freq.	%	Freq.	%
"Yes"	99	5.54	97	16.6	201	16.88	87	8.7	90	8.81
"No (but might in the future)"	1,688*	94.46	115	19.04	285	23.93	304	30.4	345	33.76
"No (would never)"	NA	NA	377	62.42	709	59.53	600	60	517	50.59
"Don't know"	0	0	10	1.66	76	6.38	5	0.5	46	4.50
No answer	NA	NA	5	0.83	31	2.6	4	0.4	24	2.35
Total	1,787	100	604	100	1,191	100	1,000	100	1,022	100

*In Turkey, the questions contained only yes or no answers, without elaboration about the future.

TABLE 6.5 Answers to "Have You Ever Been an Online Activist?"

	Turkey		Palestine		Tunisia		Lebanon		Morocco	
	Freq.	%	Freq.	%	Freq.	%	Freq.	%	Freq.	%
"Yes"	101	5.64	115	19.04	84	7.05	82	8.2	104	10.18
"Never (but might become one)"			113	18.71	291	24.43	286	28.2	267	26.13
"No (would never)"	1,686	94.35	361	59.77	709	59.53	622	62.2	579	56.65
"Don't know"	N/A	N/A	11	1.82	76	6.38	8	0.8	45	4.40
No answer	N/A	N/A	4	0.66	31	2.6	6	0.6	27	2.64
Total	1,787	100	604	100	1,191	100	1,000	100	1,022	100

young people who were previously members of protest movements, in addition to those who were members of civil society organizations like NGOs, were essential in helping others to acquire organizational skills, engage in political discourse, and build solidarity networks. Young people belonging to protest movements also argued that social media had become essential in their strategies. For them, online activism and street activism completed and complemented each other.[35] Even though a large part of the literature argues that civil society is a force for authoritarian resilience in the region, these examples demonstrate that young people can easily change from being co-opted by the regime to becoming in opposition, when they have the social capital that helps and provides them with networks of trust among different actors.

The regime's response to these mobilizational efforts, however, was repressive, and after four days of public protest and a sit-in at the park, the police used extensive force against activists. In response, mobilizations and protest continued, and a demonstration and sit-in against a policy to abolish the park turned into a protest against the AKP's policies as a whole.[36] The response to this consisted mostly of repression and violence against more than 8,000 protesters. Many of them lost their jobs and others were imprisoned.[37]

Young people who belonged to leftist and revolutionary organizations have argued that the regime normally marginalizes young people, especially those from Kurdish or leftist backgrounds. Nevertheless, if these young people mobilized for public protests, or took to the streets to mobilize others to their cause, the security forces repressed them.[38]

The Lebanese government's response to the al-Hirak, mainly the #YouStink movement, was another example of how MENA regimes dealt with a perceived threat. In the aftermath of the Arab uprisings, young people in Lebanon developed new participatory modes, such as initiatives and campaigns, in addition to starting online campaigns against certain regime policies. A large number of these were antisectarian in nature. For example, youth activists took to the streets to denounce corruption in the sectarian political system. An important case was al-Hirak, which mobilized citizens in Beirut to demonstrate against the Ministry of Environment's handling of the mounting garbage on the streets. The movement then turned from the issue of garbage to that of corruption and governance in general. A few days into the demonstrations, it added other political demands like calling for parliamentary elections, reliable basic services, and the accountability of the political elite, whether in the March 8th camp (led by Hizballah) or the March 14th camp (led by Hariri). When the police used harsh measures against al-Hirak members and demonstrators, al-Hirak fought back on social media by denouncing the actions of the security forces. Young activists uploaded many videos and photos, which later helped them build court cases to pressure the regime to release imprisoned youth. Nevertheless, the regime continued harassing al-Hirak activists until the movement's fragmentation a few months later. An important strategy utilized by the regime was a series of accusations against the movement's leaders. Among others, the main accusation from the state was that al-Hirak leaders were agents of foreign governments. Such an accusation raised questions in Lebanon's media about the sources of al-Hirak's funding, which tarnished the movement's image in society.[39]

In Morocco, large demonstrations during the Arab uprisings were sparked by the mobilizations of the February 20th youth movement, which was usually referred to simply as the "youth movement."[40] The movement was composed of groups from opposition forces, which belonged to different ideological tendencies ranging from left-wing and radical left-wing parties to Islamists that were not tolerated by the regime, like al Adl wal-Ihsan (Justice and Benevolence). Young people who participated in the February 20th movement, in addition to those who were members of human rights organizations and student unions, contended that the regime utilized excessive repression against them.[41] For instance, the regime forbade student union members from conducting opposition activities on university campuses, and as a result many young people have since refrained from protest activities.[42] Thus, as in Egypt and Lebanon, the Moroccan regime developed a counterdiscourse against young activists. In 2011, it immediately portrayed young activists as unpatriotic citizens who sympathized with the Western Sahara independence organization Polisario Front, and who were religiously immoral and unbelievers.[43] Repression against youth activists in the February 20th movement was extreme.[44]

In the OPT, young people fought different battles, and yet those who mobilized and protested against the Israeli occupation were repressed by both the Israeli authorities and the PA. Many independent movements and initiatives developed outside the mainstream NGOs. Some campaigns have been seen by the Israeli government as a threat, like the weekly protests that began in 2002 against the building of the security wall by the Israeli government. This developed into the Stop the Wall movement, which established a website documenting Israeli human rights abuses.[45] On the other hand, activism against the PA has also been present, and the PA, like the other MENA regimes, has countered it with repression. For instance, during the fieldwork with student union members at Birzeit University, the researchers found that the union consisted mainly of young people who followed different party lines, which is noteworthy because university elections are considered to be a reflection of Palestinian political sentiments. Since 2014, a pro-Hamas bloc has been winning student union elections in Birzeit University.[46] The regime does not crack down on these elections, but when young people demonstrate against the PA's strategies in Gaza, for example, repression against them increases.

In October 2015 a new surge of "revolutionary" zeal was observed among young people still in school, who were born after the 1993 Oslo Accords. The young began to call for the end of the occupation. Young people in this wave were independent; having a tendency to support one or another political faction, they were generally against political parties and were afraid that the parties would try to "ride their wave."[47]

An obstacle to young people's activism and influence on the public sphere in the OPT, however, is the PA's authoritarian structure. One young activist maintained that the previous prime minister, Salam

Fayyad, was worried that the Arab Spring might travel to the OPT. This fear led to increased suppression of youth who belonged to the political opposition, even more so than during the 1990s.[48] In 2018, for instance, when demonstrations against the Gaza blockage were held in Ramallah, police brutality led to a large number of protesters being hospitalized, while others were imprisoned.[49]

Young people who participate through mobilization for street contention and through unconventional means (like online mobilization through social networking websites) are also interested in reforming their respective regimes. Only young people in Lebanon seem to be most interested in overhauling the whole sectarian system, upon which their regime is built. Nevertheless, al-Hirak in Lebanon started as a mobilization movement to call for the attainment of basic welfare and services, access to public space, an end to the privatization process of the coastline, and the accountability of the March 8th and March 14th camps. This then culminated into calls for overhauling the system.[50] Many young people who prefer to participate through demonstrations and independent activism believe that they should sustain "a culture of activism and street demonstrations, to keep their rights of political participation alive."[51] Hence, their main objective, like that of the hope, is mainly to be included in their polity and advance freedoms, reform, and development.

Youth Precarities

The lives of young people in the MENA region have been characterized by "profound and multi-dimensional *insecurity*, although this is experienced differently according to the specificities of intersectional identities."[52] Insecurities abound, from the workplace, to lack of human rights, to increasingly having to rely on extended families and friends for social networks to find employment opportunities. The transition from school to work was experienced negatively by the majority of young people in our sample, and the surveys revealed high unemployment levels, much higher than international averages. In 2017, the overall average international youth unemployment rate was 13 percent, while in the Arab world it was almost 30 percent, making it the highest in all world regions.[53] In Turkey, youth unemployment increased from 13 percent in the year 2000 to almost 21 percent in 2017.[54] Even young people who did have a job experienced many problems and insecurities in their work. The P2Y survey showed that the majority of employed young people did not have a formal contract. These range from 17 percent in the OPT to 40 percent in Lebanon. Access to health insurance is only minimal; in Morocco, for instance, only 11 percent of young people have health insurance. A large majority of young people work in dangerous or unpleasant conditions. For instance, in Lebanon 24 percent and in the OPT 52 percent have said that they work in physically dangerous conditions.

Most young people were afraid to lose their jobs.[55] Some argued that "there's not a lot of opportunities. We can work hard and get good grades but someone who lacks competence will get the job because of wasta."[56] A young woman in Nablus said, "I feel pessimistic about jobs. I graduated. Everyone needs an intermediary, for every opportunity, for work, you need wasta in these times . . . no wasta, no work. Even for training, you are supposed to get experience, but the training doesn't help you get a job, only wasta."[57]

The P2Y survey results revealed greater material dependence on family, friends, and solidarity networks, as the various states moved away from welfare systems.[58] In all countries under analysis, the main means of finding a job was through family and friends.[59] Other studies on youth in the region have found profound differences between young people today and their parents, in terms of employment and social precarities. For instance, in the older generation (those who grew up in the 1970s and 1980s), civil servants and full-time employees constituted the majority of employed youth. Today in contrast, these same jobs are occupied by only one-quarter of young people, while the majority of employed young people are working under unstable and precarious working conditions.[60] Precarity is not exclusively linked to poverty, though it increases with poverty. Economic stagnation in the MENA region has had its toll on downward social mobility, which affects all social classes. The decreasing levels of public-sector jobs are associated with the loss of social assistance and welfare from the regime, while social security is rarely prevalent.[61] The private sector in the region, like in Egypt, does not fill the precarity gap, but it exacerbates the problem, since the governments in the region do not pressure the private sector to promote social securities.

In Morocco and Tunisia, for instance, the regimes provided young people with training and internship programs in private companies. They also offered them incentives to develop private enterprises through methods such as microcredit schemes. "These incentives however, failed to provide youth with long-term and good quality jobs, as they were instrumental in promoting the neo-liberal model of reform."[62] A young participant in Morocco's focus group explained that he completed an internship in a private company, but his "working conditions did not correspond to what the law stipulates. The labour code speaks about a provisional contract for two years but companies do not respect it."[63]

Youth Poverty

Young people in the region are among the most precariat and marginalized social groups, yet these precarities and insecurities are most pronounced for the poor, especially those who have the lowest education levels. Though employment levels are higher among the young people with less than secondary education, these young people are actually experiencing most precarities compared to their higher-educated peers. Insecurity is increasing precariousness on all fronts for the poor.[64]

Even though only a minority of young people have access to formal work contracts, these are mainly among young people who have post-secondary education levels. In Morocco, for instance, only 36 percent of young people have access to health insurance. The difference between

TABLE 6.6 Access to Health Insurance in Morocco

	"Yes, from employer"	"Yes, from other source"	"No"	Total	Sample size
Total	29	7	64	100	495
Type of living area					
Urban	41	9	50	100	302
Rural	10	5	85	100	193
Gender					
Male	29	8	63	100	337
Female	29	6	65	100	158
Highest education completed					
Less than basic	6	2	92	100	125
Preparatory/basic	17	6	77	100	119
Secondary	42	7	51	100	165
Postsecondary	55	19	26	100	86

those who are educated and those who are not is stark: 55 percent of highly educated young people have access to health insurance from their employer, compared to only 6 percent of those with less than basic education (table 6.6).

In Lebanon, more young people, at 53 percent, have access to health insurance. However, the variance between those who are educated and those who are not is also stark: 55 percent of highly educated youth have access to health insurance from their employer, compared to only 5 percent of the less educated youth (table 6.7). In Turkey, for instance, only 33 percent of young people have access to work contracts. Of these, 56 percent are youth with postsecondary education, compared to 12 percent with less than basic education (table 6.8).

Young people in Tunisia and Turkey argued that youth in peripheral rural and coastal areas were at a disadvantage in employment fields, primarily because they did not receive proper education and training.[65] In Turkey, although youth unemployment is a major public policy

TABLE 6.7 Access to Health Insurance in Lebanon

	"Yes, from employer"	"Yes, from other source"	"No"	Total	Sample size
Total	38	15	47	100	372
Type of living area					
Urban	39	15	46	100	281
Rural	35	16	49	100	91
Gender					
Male	40	13	47	100	265
Female	31	24	45	100	107
Highest education completed					
Less than basic	5	8	87	100	35
Preparatory/ basic	24	8	68	100	86
Secondary	32	21	47	100	65
Postsecondary	55	19	26	100	186

TABLE 6.8 Access to a Written Work Contract in Turkey

	Yes	No	Total	Sample size
Total	33	67	100	701
Type of living area				
Urban	33	67	100	648
Rural	26	74	100	53
Gender				
Male	31	69	100	482
Female	37	63	100	219
Highest education completed				
Less than basic	12	88	100	62
Preparatory/ basic	21	79	100	154
Secondary	28	72	100	266
Postsecondary	56	44	100	219

concern as well as a concern of young people, only rarely have any youth initiatives or organizations tackled this problem.[66] Young people who belonged to civil society organizations were mainly concerned with social development and equity in their respective regimes. There was a strong tendency to try to help other young people in marginalized and rural areas. Young people often criticized their governments for ineffective development policies and for corrupt systems that favored development projects in urban areas and large cities, while neglecting rural areas and peripheral cities.[67] Moroccan focus-group participants claimed that there was unequal access to state services and employment opportunities. Clientelism infested the political system and did not encourage upward social mobility.[68] Inequalities increased between young people in poor urban areas and those in big cities where jobs were concentrated. The export-oriented policies promoted by the Tunisian government increased the marginalization of farmers. "[Farmers] offered a low-cost manpower on which firms on coastal cities could draw, increasing labour insecurity conditions, while women, including young women, increasingly took the place of young men working on family farms and in agro-business companies at very low wages."[69]

In addition to these deeply felt problems and insecurities among young people in these MENA regimes, the repressive capabilities of the regimes, especially against youth who were marginalized, "mean that personal and physical insecurity is pervasive for young people and especially for young women." Some young women argued, "We have to psychologically prepare ourselves for going out." Others said, "If someone well-connected hurts you, you can do nothing . . . and everyone is well-connected." One added, "Even when I go out with my friends and we are four girls, I still do not feel safe." A Tunisian respondent said, "It is as simple as not having anything to fear. As a young woman I think I would be fully safe if I could go out at night and have a stroll without needing to fear anything, without fearing being raped or killed or robbed." A Palestinian female remarked, "We are safe only in our families."[70]

Perceptions of Reform and Change

All young people—those who are perceived as either the hope or the threat—are influenced by the global neoliberal discourse of development. Many believe in the importance of market-led development, which is supported by the IFIs. Youth empowerment for these young people is mainly based on educational reform and smooth school-to-work transitions. Young people do not feel that they influence public policies concerning employment and education. They believe that the main impediment to attaining these developments is cronyism and corruption in their respected regimes. This corruption plays out differently depending on the political context in each regime. However, ultimately corruption tainted the society of all the MENA nations in the P2Y. The closure of the public sphere and the increasing use of repression are also main concerns of young people, especially young activists. Nevertheless, the young display more interests in "reform" from within the system than revolution. The most "revolutionary" demands were made by young Lebanese activists who wanted to abolish the well-established political sectarian system.[71] For those who are engaged through protest activities, boycotting formal institutions and street demonstrations for them are the only ways that regimes would listen to their grievances.

Youth who are civically and politically engaged advance change through the formal institutional structures and can demonstrate how hope or loyalty could turn into threat or exit and voice. The majority of young engaged people manifested their interest in social, cultural, and political participation within the confines of the status quo and current political structure. They preferred and accepted working in this way to try and realize their aspirations of social, economic, and political inclusion. They accepted the general laws, traditions, and cultures of their respective polities. They wanted to reform these polities but without a complete overhaul of existing structures. Nevertheless, they have also voiced their concerns about and dissatisfaction with the system even though they themselves seem to thrive in it.

There was a strong tendency among those representing the promise in the sample to criticize their regimes for the lack of political freedoms. Young people who belonged to political parties, mainly in Morocco, Tunisia, and Turkey, tended to be critical of their regimes' policies in regard to opposition parties and activists. Although they believed in evolutionary change through the political system, they argued that the current regimes were not receptive to including youth in the decision-making and governance processes. Many young people in the sample said that due to their regimes' shortcomings and imminent unemployment problems they would rather emigrate to find better job opportunities. One young Palestinian explained that "one third of young people are thinking of emigration as an alternative to living in a society where they cannot participate." Another added, "if we could, we would all move!"[72] If these young people do not exit, and cannot find proper channels for migration, they could turn into "voice" or threat.

Conclusion

This chapter briefly analyzed young people in five MENA countries besides Egypt. It demonstrated the extent to which the hope/promise, the threat/peril, and the marginalized/poor live under similar conditions in the majority of these countries. The dynamics of neoliberal developments in the region have classified young people into the dichotomous understanding of youth for development and empowerment, or more securitized discourses. Although the regimes have fostered the development of civil society organizations and have included in them young people that are perceived as the hope, it is evident that these young people, even when they are co-opted into the sociopolitical and economic structures, could turn into a perceived threat when faced with no viable alternatives.

An interesting example in this case is of young people who participated in the Gezi Park demonstrations. The majority of activists at Gezi Park were civically engaged in various civil society organizations, and they developed networks of trust among one another, which helped in shaping and developing their sustained demonstrations. Young people belonging to subaltern groups—those who are marginalized—in particular experienced immense insecurities, not only because of their political participation through unconventional means against their respective regimes, but also because it was not easy to find decent employment and a good standard of living without the necessary social networks of wasta.

Some young people would prefer to migrate but were confronted by another set of security controls from countries in the north that restrict migration; hence many have found little opportunity of exiting their countries. Their remaining options have been either to try to reform incrementally the socioeconomic and political systems under which they live or to abstain from political and civic participation, as was shown in the quantitative analysis. Or finally, they could try and influence change through revolutionary means. The precariousness and insecurity under which these young people live had exposed the thin lines among the hope/loyalty, threat/voice, and marginalized/exit groups.

Conclusion

This book examined the role of youth in the political transformation of contemporary Egypt through an analysis of politics from above and below. It discussed the relationship between the political economy of authoritarianism and the daily struggles of young people living within this structure. It examined the questions of how half a century of authoritarianism and securitization, coupled with economic reforms and neoliberalism, has affected the lives of young people today. It discussed young people's major issues and concerns and how these concerns alter state-society relations and contribute to social change and continuity.

The political economy of youth approach focuses on the causes of the economic trends and their effects on the living standards of young people.[1] The strength of this approach is its identification of the roots of the political positioning of young people within a market-oriented economy. It distinguishes between the degree of attention paid to the relationship between the position of young people within a polity, and the totality of the social relations that make up the economy, including the political, social, and cultural areas of life. It traces the long-term patterns of social changes and continuities.[2] The ongoing debate about this approach has mainly been analyzed in democratic contexts, especially in the developed north. This book contributes to this ongoing debate through analyzing this approach in an authoritarian context in the developing south. The main objective of this book has been to understand the extent to which authoritarian, securitized and neoliberal contexts have shaped and constrained the daily lives and struggles of young people today.

The Political Economy of Youth: An Approach from Above

The first part of this book discussed the structure of the political economy in Egypt, as well as the regime's framing of young people. Chapter 1 analyzed the political dynamics of the Nasser regime, which embedded a deep state built on patron-client relations that became the foundation of subsequent regimes. Although the economic development model moved from Import Substitution and Industrialization to an open market economy, leading to a neoliberal system of sorts, the social dynamics in Egypt have sustained a political economy based on authoritarianism and securitization. This relationship has been dynamic throughout the past six decades, with economic elites gradually switching allegiance from one sociopolitical group to another according to their interests. Nevertheless, power relations within the polity have remained the same. Corruption, cronyism, and patron-client relations have continued intact, even if the elite or the persons involved may have changed. For example, the authoritarian regimes of Mubarak and al-Sisi shifted their relationship with the economic elite from a provision pact to a protection pact. The first pact relies on the support of elites by providing them with monetary perks like jobs, public funds, and state contracts. The second pact relies on a "shared sense of threat," where different elite members give their support to the regime to protect themselves from serious challenges to their property, their privileges, or their personal safety.[3] The role of the military has also substantially changed since the Sadat regime. While Sadat decreased the role of military personnel, al-Sisi reversed this. Today, almost 67 percent of provincial governors are from military backgrounds, compared to 44 percent under Mubarak and almost 20 percent under Sadat.[4]

Economic reform, especially since Sadat's presidency, has been tightly linked with securitizing the regime. Chapter 1 demonstrated that the present authoritarian, securitized, neoliberal system could not have been implemented without reliance on the security forces. Repression and co-optation of young people have remained the primary strategies of subsequent regimes to fend off dissent and to maintain authoritarianism.

Chapter 2 discussed the framing and discourse toward young people by Egypt's rulers from Nasser until al-Sisi. Because young people experience historical events in a different manner from older generations, their perceptions of the polity are valuable. This difference is important for the direction of social change within a polity. The historical analysis of youth worldwide has referred to their position within the polity as *hope* of the nation for development, as opposed to the concept of youth as a *threat* to the social and economic order. In the contemporary era of globalization and neoliberalization, youth have been referred to from a positivist perspective as partners in development. However, they have also increasingly been perceived as a threat to the status quo. When nation-states enter times of crisis, a moral panic tends to ensue where either a person or group becomes defined as a threat to the social values and interests of the nation.[5] Since the 1950s, rulers in Egypt and in other Middle East and North Africa (MENA) countries have always portrayed their position in time and space as living in a permanent crisis.

The crises have been constructed either through external enemies, international wars, regional wars, or dire economic straits. The major group of persons perceived as a *threat* to the nation have been young people, in particular those in the political opposition and those who have the capacity to mobilize others for public demonstrations. Chapter 2 elaborated on the perception and framing of young people by various regimes, how they have co-opted some youth into their ranks, how their discourse has revolved around political development, and how they want young people to be on their side. Concurrently, young people positioned at the oppositional end of the political spectrum have the will and capacity to demonstrate against the regimes either on political issues like the 1967 war defeat or economic issues like the 1977 bread riots. However, these young people have been actively repressed by the regime.

The Political Economy of Youth: An Approach from Below

This book also sought to identify young people's own role in shaping, organizing, and legitimating the social, economic, and political structures in their polity.[6] To understand these dynamics, I clustered youth into three categories: the promise/hope, the peril/threat, and the poor/marginalized. These categories were taken from three major trends in youth studies: the liberal, the securitization, and the critical political economy trends.

The first trend—the liberal perspective—analyzes youth within the context of positivity, where scholars and policy makers have generally perceived young people as positive agents for development. They have identified "the core competencies and characteristics that youth need to have to develop into healthy and 'thriving' adults in a 'free' and 'productive' society and economy."[7] The hope of the nation are those young people who fall within this positive and hopeful category.

This group are the youth who grew up accepting and becoming integrated into the globalized neoliberal era, and who became an integral part of the development process as defined by international financial institutions and the United Nations Development Programme (UNDP). They joined the increasing number and scope of mainstream civil society actors. Young people in this category are manifestations of the hope within an authoritarian political economy. They believe in their power to effect change, they understand that they can add to the development of their society, and they are keen to establish organizations and initiatives to enhance economic development in their respective countries and to promote the inclusion of young people in the public sphere. They perceive themselves as reformers of their nation's future.

Yet these same young people are increasingly constricted by society at large, by the surge of repression, and by the political elite's closure of the public sphere. They have voiced their interest and enthusiasm for socioeconomic and political change, through their formal participation in the civic and political spheres. Nevertheless, they have also voiced their discontent with their marginalization in mainstream political and civil society organizations. They have also shown frustration at the increasingly shrinking public space, which constrains their goals for more freedoms and reform. These young people represent loyalty that could turn into voice and/or exit.[8]

During the fieldwork discussed in chapters 3 and 4, young people expressed how they developed their own "parallel universe" to establish their ideal participatory patterns. They also discussed why they decided to disengage, or to change, their patterns of engagement. They articulated their frustration with their political regime, which does not permit street activities, whether in the form of carnivals, sporting events, public awareness campaigns, or demonstrations. Although youth who are perceived as the hope have been co-opted by the regime and have high stakes in developing and reforming the polity from within the authoritarian structure, they could at times shift to become voice if they felt unacceptably constrained in achieving their desired goals. They could also turn to voice if and when exit became impossible.

The second trend of youth analysis is the securitization approach, which focuses on youth as a threat to the social order. For instance, the increase in population and the youth bulge are threats to development in a polity. Young people's potential to mobilize for dissent and to demonstrate is also perceived as a security threat by authoritarian regimes.[9] In addition, the growing number of young people longing to migrate to the north is perceived as a national security threat by northern countries, the European Union and the United States in particular.

For the purposes of this analysis, I identified those young people who mobilize and demonstrate for dissent as the threat to the nation. This threat in Egypt was discussed in chapter 4, and the threat in the MENA region was analyzed in chapter 6. These young people mostly align with the political opposition and mobilize for dissent either through joining different protest movements, establishing their own protest movements, founding human rights organizations, joining nontolerated political parties, or simply becoming independent political activists. The majority of young people in this category prefer to voice their dissent through street contention and social networking sites. It is important to note, however, that the surveys conducted in the six countries in the Power2-Youth project indicate that although online activism is indeed common, it is not as common as street contention. For many young activists, particularly in Egypt, their presence on the street to work with people, to mobilize them or to develop public awareness campaigns, seems to have been more important than online activism.

Regime repression in Egypt and the other five countries under analysis was highest toward the youth who, from their regimes' perspective, represented the threat to the nation. These young people were believed to disrupt the political and social structures through their political engagement. This was most notable in Lebanon, whose regime is among the least autocratic or is at least partly free according to Freedom House's classification.[10]

Young people who called for an end to the sectarian political system and mobilized others toward that during the 2015 al-Hirak demonstration suffered the most. The media machine delegitimized them while the police repressed them. Young people in this category, however, do not perceive themselves as a threat: they also believe that they are reformers of the current socioeconomic and political system. The majority of them have argued that, most of the time, they cannot change the current socioeconomic and political stalemate from conventional forms of participation, since these organizations tend to marginalize youth in the decision-making process. They believe that they can change only through street contention and independent activism. They were most likely to exit not only through migration, but also through ceasing their civic and political participation. More importantly, however, is the discussion in chapter 4 about the fact that young people can become more violent and radicalized when repression increases.[11]

The third trend in youth studies—the critical political economy approach—is linked to the second but is more critical of the neoliberal structure in which the global economy is situated. This trend argues that there should be a more nuanced analysis of the precarity and unemployment, as well as consideration of other factors that cause this precarity. "In many societies, dominant political and economic power sources are closely aligned, and governments therefore have a tendency to develop policies favouring those with economic power, while ignoring or undermining the interests of those without economic power."[12]

The main thrust of chapter 5 and the latter part of chapter 6 shed light on the life experiences of these ignored or marginalized youth. The dichotomy of how the regimes in Egypt and in the MENA region have marginalized, yet also repressed a large number of young uneducated, poor, and subaltern groups, is pointed out. The analysis highlights how market-oriented reforms and neoliberal policies are inseparable from the use of force. Chapter 5 discussed the extent to which the Mubarak and al-Sisi regimes developed market-oriented reforms that directly threatened the living standards of young people, especially those already trapped in low standards of living. It confirmed that education is intimately linked to better life chances; nevertheless, it demonstrates that family income levels are more important in increasing young people's life chances than education. The quantitative and qualitative analysis showed that if a young person came from a low standard of living, has low education levels and had no networks of privilege and access to "wasta," his or her life chances were much lower than those of a young person at the same educational level, but whose family enjoyed a better standard of living. While youth precarity and feelings of insecurity have increased, the regime has escalated its use of repression against these marginalized young people.

The neoliberal economic policies in the region have given rise to a dichotomy in which young people from low-income families are marginalized from basic infrastructure, welfare provisions, and opportunities for better life chances, while greater repression is applied against the poor, marginalized, and subaltern groups for fear that they could turn into voice. These marginalized young people perceive themselves to be marginalized and excluded within the polity. They have mostly chosen to exit the formal economic structures and institutions and have found other informal structures on which to depend, such as informal economic sectors and informal settlements. They have also chosen to exit the public sphere, so that very few are politically engaged in formal politics or civil society. Nevertheless, like other young people, they could choose to voice their discontent through demonstrations and contestations against their respective regimes if repression and marginalization become intolerable.

This book has attempted to situate young people in Egypt and the MENA region within the framework of global youth studies. The analysis of youth as the promise, the peril, and the poor seeks to contribute to international debates on the role of youth in this era of global neoliberal transformations, in addition to understanding the dynamics of change and continuity in today's Egypt.

ACKNOWLEDGMENTS

I'm thankful to many colleagues, friends, and family. Most importantly I'm grateful for all young people who agreed to be part of our research project, either through interviews or focus groups or simply by participating in our different events. Their stories, insights, and passion for Egypt are indescribable.

The fieldwork for the book was part of an EUFP7 research project, Power2Youth. I'm indebted to Daniela Pioppi and Maria Cristina Paciello for inviting me to be part of this project. I'm grateful to my research team in Cairo, Rana Gaber, Hatem Zayed, Batoul al-Mehdar, Mayar El Zanaty and Alia Alaa Eddin, without whom the research project would not have seen light. Their enthusiasm, interest, and hard work throughout the project have inspired me. I'm also thankful to all research teams in our partner universities and research centers who were part of this project. Our debates, workshops, and discussions throughout our research journey have influenced my thoughts and research. I'm most thankful to Emma Murphy for our endless discussions on the political economy of youth and for her help throughout the journey. I'm thankful to Åge Tiltnes for sharing the raw data of all surveys with me and for helping me with the analysis. My thoughts have also been influenced and shaped by discussions with Robert MacDonald, Daniela Pioppi, and Emma Murphy during our writing workshop in Rome in 2018.

My utmost gratitude goes to Lisa Anderson who read previous drafts of the manuscript and provided me with insightful comments and suggestions. I'm also thankful for Lovise Aalen for inviting me to the workshop on Youth, Inequality and Regime Response in the Global South at the Chr. Michelsen Institute in Bergen, where I discussed some chapters and received insightful comments from all participants. The blind reviewers of the manuscript gave very interesting and helpful comments to crisp my arguments and analysis. I hope the final version of the book is up to their expectations. I'm grateful to Sonia Tsuruoka, my editor at New York University Press, for her enthusiasm and interest in this book. Her help and support are very much appreciated. I would like to thank Virginia Myers for editing the earlier draft of the book. I would also like to thank Sean Hobbs for editing the final version of the book.

Last but most importantly I would like to thank my family and friends, Mary and Adel in particular, for supporting me throughout this journey, I would have never been who I am without their love, encouragement, and support. Edward, Tamer, and Celine are, of course, the backbone of this whole project.

NOTES

INTRODUCTION

1 Ronald Wintrobe, *The Political Economy of Dictatorship* (Cambridge: Cambridge University Press, 1998).

2 Robert Migdal, *The State in Society: Studying How States and Societies Transform and Constitute One Another* (Cambridge: Cambridge University Press, 2004).

3 Amr Adly, "Economic Recovery in Egypt Won't Guarantee Political Stability," Carnegie Middle East Center (May 20, 2015), http://carnegie-mec.org.

4 Zeinab Abul-Magd, "Egypt's Adaptable Officers: Business, Nationalism and Discontent," in *Businessmen in Arms: How the Military and Other Armed Groups Profit in the MENA Region*, ed. Elke Gerwart and Zeinab Abul-Magd (Lanham, MD: Rowman and Littlefield, 2016), 23–42.

5 See, for instance, Clement Henry and Robert Springborg, *Globalization and the Politics of Development in the Middle East* (Cambridge: Cambridge University Press, 2010); Robert Springborg, "The Precarious Economics of Arab Springs," *Survival: Global Politics and Strategy* 53, no. 6 (2011): 85–104; Robert Springborg, "Globalization and Its Discontents in the MENA Region," *Middle East Policy* 23, no. 2 (Summer 2016): 146–160; and Samer Soliman, *The Autumn of Dictatorship: Fiscal Crisis and Political Change in Egypt under Mubarak*, trans. Peter Daniel (Stanford, CA: Stanford University Press, 2011).

6 Migdal, *State in Society*.

7 For more discussions on "cleft capitalism," see Amr Adly, *Cleft Capitalism: The Social Origins of Failed Market Making in Egypt* (Stanford, CA: Stanford University Press, 2020). As this introduction and chapter 1 will demonstrate, the economic system under which Egypt is functioning today cannot be regarded as a "pure" neoliberal system, since the military institution is directly intervening in the market and competing with the private sector. For more accounts of the role of the military in the economy, see Zeinab Abul Magd, *Militarizing the Nation: The Army, Business and Revolution in Egypt* (New York: Columbia University Press, 2017).

8 Asef Bayat, *Life as Politics: How Ordinary People Change the Middle East*, 2nd ed. (Stanford, CA: Stanford University Press, 2013), 19.

9 James Côté, "Towards a New Political Economy of Youth," *Journal of Youth Studies* 17, no. 4 (2014): 527–543, 528.

10 James Côté, "A New Political Economy of Youth Reprised: Rejoinder to France and Threadgold," *Journal of Youth Studies* 19, no. 6 (2016): 852–868, 854.

11 Côté, "Towards a New Political Economy of Youth," 537.

12 Mayssoun Sukarieh and Stuart Tannock, "On the Political Economy of Youth: A Comment," *Journal of Youth Studies* 19, no. 9 (2016): 1281–1289, 1285.

13 Côté, "New Political Economy of Youth Reprised."

14 Lisa Wedeen, *Authoritarian Apprehensions: Ideology, Judgment, and Mourning in Syria* (Chicago: University of Chicago Press, 2019).

15 Karl Mannheim, "The Problem of Generations," in *Essays on the Sociology of Knowledge*, ed. Karl Mannheim (London: RKP, 1952).

16 Virpi Timonen and Catherine Conlon, "Beyond Mannheim: Conceptualizing How People 'Talk' and 'Do' Generations in Contemporary Society," *Advances in Life Course Research* 24 (2015): 1–9.

17 Joseph Demartini, "Change Agents and Generational Relationships: A Reevaluation of Mannheim's Problem of Generations," *Social Forces* 65, no. 1 (1985): 1–16; Jane Pilcher, "Mannheim's Sociology of Generations: An Undervalued Legacy," *British Journal of Sociology* 45, no. 3 (1994): 481–495.

18 Demartini, "Change Agents," 2.

19 Ibid.

20 Robert MacDonald, "Youth Transitions, Unemployment and Underemployment: Plus ça change, plus c'est la même chose?," *Journal of Sociology* (2011): 1–18, https://doi.org/10.1177/1440783311420794.

21 Ibid.

22 Ibid.

23 Mark Tessler, Carrie Konold, and Megan Reif, "Political Generations in Developing Countries: Evidence and Insights from Algeria," *Public Opinion Quarterly* 68, no. 2 (2004): 184–216.

24 Emma Murphy, "The In-securitisation of Youth in the South and East Mediterranean," *International Spectator* 53, no. 2 (2018): 21–37.

25 Ibid., 21. Emphasis in the original.

26 Mayssoun Sukarieh and Stuart Tannock, "The Positivity Imperative: A Critical Look at the 'New' Youth Development Movement," *Journal of Youth Studies* 14, no. 6 (2011): 675–691.

27 See, for instance, Murphy, "In-securitisation of Youth"; and Emma Murphy, "A Political Economy of Youth Policy in Tunisia," *New Political Economy* 22, no. 6 (2017): 676–691.

28 Jona Nyman, "Securitization Theory," in *Critical Approaches to Security*, ed. Laura Shepherd (London: Routledge, 2013), 51–62; Maysoon Sukarieh and Stuart Tannock, "The Global Securitization of Youth," *Third World Quarterly* (2017): 854–870.

29 Sukarieh and Tannock, "Global Securitization of Youth."

30 Assefa Mehretu, Bruce William Pigozzi, and Lawrence M. Sommers, "Concepts in Social and Spatial Marginality," *Geografiska Annaler, Series B Human Geography* 82 B (2000): 89–101, 91.

31 Diane Singerman, "Youth, Gender, and Dignity in the Egyptian Uprising," *Journal of Middle East Women's Studies* 9, no. 3 (2013): 1–27, 8.

32 Michael Hoffman and Amaney Jamal, "The Youth and the Arab Spring: Cohort Differences and Similarities," *Middle East Law and Governance* 4 (2012): 168–188.

33 Côté, "New Political Economy of Youth Reprised," 862.

34 Albert Hirschman, *Exit, Voice and Loyalty: Responses to Decline in Firms, Organizations, and States* (Cambridge, MA: Harvard University Press, 1970); Albert Hirschman, " 'Exit, Voice and Loyalty': Further Reflections and a Survey of Recent Contributions," *Milbank Memorial Fund Quarterly: Health and Society* 58, no. 3 (1980): 430–453.

35 Hirschman, *Exit, Voice and Loyalty*.

36 Côté, "New Political Economy of Youth Reprised," 854.

37 Edward Sayre, "Labor Force Conditions of Middle East Youth: The Role of Demographics, Institutions, and Gender in the Arab Uprisings," in *Political and Socio-Economic Change in the Middle East and North Africa: Gender Perspectives and Survival Strategies*, ed. Roksana Bahramitash and Hadi Salehi Esfahani (New York: Palgrave Macmillan, 2016), 75–98. For more discussions on manufacturing consent in other parts of the world, see Edward Herman and Noam Chomsky, *Manufacturing Consent: The Political Economy of the Mass Media* (London: Bodley Head, 2008).

38 Bayat, *Life as Politics*, 19.

39 Mayssoun Sukarieh and Stuart Tannock, *Youth Rising? The Politics of Youth in the Global Economy* (London: Routledge, 2015).

40 Ibid., 4.

41 Nadine Sika, "Civil Society and the Rise of Unconventional Modes of Political Participation," *Middle East Law and Governance* 10, no. 3 (2019): 237–263.

42 See, for instance, Mona Harb, "Youth Mobilization in Lebanon: Navigating Exclusion and Seeds for Collective Action," Power2Youth working paper no. 16 (October 3, 2016), http://power2youth.iai.it/publications/youth-mobilisation-in -lebanon-navigating-exclusion-and-seeds-for-collective-action.html (accessed July 1, 2018); and Birzeit University, "Organizational Factors of Youth Exclusion in the Occupied Palestinian Territories," Power2Youth working paper no. 22 (December 9, 2016), http://power2youth.iai.it/publications/organizational-factors-of-youth -exclusion-and-inclusion-in-the-occupied-palestinian-territories.html (accessed July 5, 2018). See also Saloua Zerhouni and Azeddine Akesbi, "Youth Activism in Morocco: Exclusion, Agency and the Search for Inclusion," Power2Youth working paper no. 15 (September 2016), www.iai.it/sites/default/files/p2y_15.pdf (accessed July 22, 2018).

43 Amaney Jamal, *Barriers to Democracy: The Other Side of Social Capital in Palestine and the Arab World* (Princeton, NJ: Princeton University Press, 2007); Justin Gengler, Mark Tessler, Darwish Al-Emadi, and Abdoulaye Diop, "Civic Life and Democratic Citizenship in Qatar: Findings from the First Qatar World Values Survey," *Middle East Law and Governance* 5, no. 3 (2013): 258–279.

44 Maha Abdel Rahman, "The Politics of 'Uncivil' Society in Egypt," *Review of African Political Economy* 29, no. 91 (2002): 21–35.

45 Harb, "Youth Mobilization in Lebanon." See also Nadine Sika, "Beyond the Impasse? Dynamics of Youth Agency in Times of Crisis," Mediterranean Politics 26, no. 3 (2021): 273–284.

46 Ali Akyüz, Gümüş Pınar, Volkan Yılmaz, and Ferhat Mahir Çakaloz, "Youth Exclusion and the Transformative Impact of Youth in Turkey," Power2Youth working paper no. 2 (October 26, 2016), http://power2youth.iai.it/publications /youth-exclusion-and-the-transformative-impact-of-organized-youth-in-turkey. html (accessed July 18, 2018). See also Sika, "Beyond the Impasse?"

47 Holger Albrecht, ed., *Contentious Politics in the Middle East: Political Opposition under Authoritarianism* (Gainesville, FL: University of Florida Press, 2010).

48 Michael Mann, *Fascists* (Cambridge, MA: Cambridge University Press, 2004).

49 Sukarieh and Tannock, *Youth Rising?*

50 Jamal, *Barriers to Democracy.*

51 Sika, "Civil Society."

52 Amy Hawthorne, "Middle Eastern Democracy: Is Civil Society the Answer?" *Carnegie Endowment for International Peace* (March 2004), https://carnegieen dowment.org (accessed July 22, 2018).

53 For more information about the research project in each country, see Power2Youth: Freedom, Dignity and Justice, http://power2youth.iai.it/index.html.

54 The qualitative analysis is based on five focus groups, each with four to seven participants and thirty-three semistructured interviews with young civil society actors, ranging from members of protest movements, civil society organizations, and political parties, to independent activists, between April 2015 and April 2016. Analysis of them is based on a total of thirty-six partici-pants, twenty-six of whom were male and ten of whom were females. The interviews were held between May and November 2015 with twenty-one young men and thirteen young women whose average age was twenty-five. The majority of the interviewees (twenty-three) reside in Cairo, have a bachelor's degree (twenty-one) and had attended public tertiary education (twenty-four). The quantitative analysis is based on a random sample survey of 1,200 young Egyptians undertaken in April 2016. The questionnaire was designed by the P2Y partners, and the survey was also conducted in Turkey, Lebanon, Palestine, Tunisia, Morocco, and Egypt. For more information on the qualitative fieldwork, see Nadine Sika, "Varieties of Youth Civic and Political Engagement in the South East of the

Mediterranean: A Comparative Analysis," working paper no. 23 (2017), www
.iai.it/sites/default/files/p2y_23.pdf.

55 Sukarieh and Tannock, "On the Political Economy of Youth," 1285.

56 Ibid., 1284.

57 Ibid., 1283.

58 Peter Kelly, "Three Notes on a Political Economy of Youth," *Journal of Youth
Studies* 21, no. 10 (2018): 1283–1304, 1292.

59 Adel Abdel Ghaffar, *Egyptians in Revolt: The Political Economy of Labor and
Student Mobilizations 1919–2011* (London: Routledge, 2017).

60 Ibid.

61 Kelly, "Three Notes," 1294.

62 Ibid., 1295.

63 This part builds on the literature on youth, in which Sukarieh and Tannock argue
that youth studies have rarely analyzed "the question of how young people and
youth . . . play a role in shaping, organizing or legitimating social, cultural,
political and economic structures and practices generally and globally." "On
the Political Economy of Youth," 1285.

CHAPTER 1. THE POLITICAL ECONOMY OF AUTHORITARIANISM IN EGYPT

1 For an overview of the whole report, see the World Bank in Egypt, "Overview,"
www.worldbank.org/en/country/egypt/overview.

2 I translated page 7 of *Al-Shorouk*. That day was wholly dedicated to the increase
in metro tariffs.

3 Koenraad Bogaert, "Contextualizing the Arab Revolts: The Politics behind Three
Decades of Neoliberalism in the Arab World," *Middle East Critique* 22, no. 3
(2013): 213–234.

4 Mitchell Dean, "Rethinking Neoliberalism," *Journal of Sociology* 50, no. 2 (2014):
150–163.

5 James Côté, "A New Political Economy of Youth Reprised: Rejoinder to France
and Threadgold," *Journal of Youth Studies* 19, no. 6 (2016): 852–868, 853.

6 More analysis of this power struggle is discussed in chapter 2.

7 Merete B. Seeberg, "Electoral Authoritarianism and Economic Control,"
International Political Science Review 39, no. 1 (2018): 33–48.

8 Robert Springborg, "Deep States in the MENA," *Middle East Policy* 25, no. 1
(Spring 2018): 136–157, 141.

9 Raymond Baker, *Sadat and After: Struggles for Egypt's Political Soul* (Cambridge,
MA: Harvard University Press, 1990).

10 Ibid.

11 Hazem Kandil, *Soldiers, Spies and Statesmen: Egypt's Road to Revolt* (London:
Verso, 2012), 64.

12 Mark Cooper, *The Transformation of Egypt* (London: Croom Helm, 1982).

13 Robert Springborg, "Patrimonialism and Policy Making in Egypt: Nasser and Sadat and the Tenure Policy for Reclaimed Land," *Middle Eastern Studies* 15, no. 5 (1979): 49–69.

14 Baker, *Sadat and After*.

15 Gilles Keppel, *Jihad: The Trail of Political Islam* (Cambridge, MA: Harvard University Press, 2002); Baker, *Sadat and After*; Adel Abdel Ghafar, *Egyptians in Revolt: The Political Economy of Labor and Student Mobilizations 1919–2011* (London: Routledge, 2017); Kandil, *Soldiers, Spies and Statesmen*.

16 Kandil, *Soldiers, Spies and Statesmen*.

17 Cooper, *Transformation of Egypt*, 70.

18 Ibid.

19 Kandil, *Soldiers, Spies and Statesmen*.

20 Zeinab Abul-Magd, "Egypt's Adaptable Officers: Business, Nationalism, and Discontent," in *Businessmen in Arms: How the Military and Other Armed Groups Profit in the MENA Region*, ed. Elke Grawert and Zeinab Abul-Magd (Lanham, MD: Rowman and Littlefield, 2016), 23–41.

21 Baker, *Sadat and After*, 16.

22 Ghafar, *Egyptians in Revolt*.

23 Allan Richards et al., *A Political Economy of the Middle East: Third Edition* (Boulder, CO: Westview Press, 2013); Ghafar, *Egyptians in Revolt*.

24 Richards et al., *Political Economy of the Middle East*.

25 Zeinab Abul-Magd, *Militarizing the Nation: The Army, Business and Revolution in Egypt* (New York: Columbia University Press, 2017).

26 Richards et al., *Political Economy of the Middle East*, 223.

27 Kandil, *Soldiers, Spies and Statesmen*.

28 Abul-Magd, "Egypt's Adaptable Officers."

29 Simon Bromley and Ray Bush, "Adjustment in Egypt? The Political Economy of Reform," *Review of African Political Economy* 21, no. 60 (1994): 201–213.

30 Richards et al., *Political Economy of the Middle East*, 240.

31 Sadiq Ahmed, *Public Finance in Egypt: Its Structure and Trends* (Washington, DC: World Bank, 1984).

32 Maha Abdelrahman, "Policing Neoliberalism in Egypt: The Continuing Rise of the Securocratic State," *Third World Quarterly* 38, no. 1 (2017): 185–202.

33 Eberhard Kienle, *A Grand Delusion: Democracy and Economic Reform in Egypt* (London: I. B. Tauris, 2000).

34 Ibid.

35 Nazih Ayubi, *Overstating the Arab State: Politics and Society in the Middle East* (London: I. B. Tauris, 1995); Raymond Hinnebush Jr., *Egyptian Politics under Sadat: The Post-Populist Development of an Authoritarian-Modernizing State* (Cambridge: Cambridge University Press, 1985).

36 Ayubi, *Overstating the Arab State*.

37 Ghafar, *Egyptians in Revolt*.

38 Abdel Azim Hammad, "Fassad lahu tarikh" [The history of corruption], *Al-Shorouk*, February 16, 2017, www.shorouknews.com (accessed April 25, 2018).

39 Springborg, "Patrimonialism and Policy Making in Egypt."

40 Ibid., 52.

41 Ibid.

42 Joshua Stacher, *Adaptable Autocrats: Regime Power in Egypt and Syria* (Stanford, CA: Stanford University Press, 2012).

43 Samer Soliman, *The Autumn of Dictatorship: Fiscal Crisis and Political Change in Egypt under Mubarak*, trans. Peter Daniel (Stanford, CA: Stanford University Press, 2011).

44 Ibid.

45 Abul-Magd, *Militarizing the Nation.*

46 Soliman, *Autumn of Dictatorship.*

47 Ibid.

48 Ibid.

49 Ibid.

50 Abul-Magd, *Militarizing the Nation.*

51 Abul-Magd, "Egypt's Adaptable Officers."

52 Ibid.

53 Ibid.

54 Yezid Sayigh, *Above the State: The Officers' Republic in Egypt*, Carnegie Papers (Washington, DC: Carnegie Middle East Center, 2012).

55 Abdelrahman, "Policing Neoliberalism in Egypt," 189–190.

56 Springborg, "Patrimonialism and Policy Making in Egypt," 149.

57 Koenraad Bogaert, "Contextualizing the Arab Revolts: The Politics behind Three Decades of Neoliberalism in the Arab World," *Middle East Critique* 22, no. 3 (2013): 213–234.

58 Amr Adly, *Cleft Capitalism: The Social Origins of Failed Market Making in Egypt* (Stanford, CA: Stanford University Press, 2020), 5.

59 Ibid., 7.

60 David Harvey, *The New Imperialism* (New York: Oxford University Press, 2003), 137.

61 Koenraad Bogaert and Montserrat Emperador, "Imagining the State through Social Protest: State Reformation and the Mobilizations of Unemployed Graduates in Morocco," *Mediterranean Politics* 16, no. 2 (2011): 241–259.

62 Paul Amar, *The Security Archipelago: Human-Security, States, Sexuality Politics and the End of Neoliberalism* (Durham, NC: Duke University Press, 2013).

63 Adam Hanieh, *Lineages of Revolt* (Chicago: Haymarket Books, 2013), 66.

64 Hamouda Chekir and Ishak Diwan, "Crony Capitalism in Egypt," *Journal of Globalization and Development* 5, no. 2 (2014): 177–211.

65 Abdelrahman, "Policing Neoliberalism in Egypt."

66 African Development Bank Group, "Egypt: Economic Reform and Structural Adjustment Programme: Project Performance Evaluation" (2000), www.afdb .org/fileadmin/uploads/afdb/Documents/Evaluation-Reports-_Shared-With -OPEV_/05092259-EN-EGYPT-ECONOMIC-REFORM-AND-SAP.PDF (accessed July 15, 2018).

67 Joseph Sassoon, *Anatomy of Authoritarianism in Arab Republics* (Cambridge: Cambridge University Press, 2016).

68 Maha Abdelrahman, *Egypt's Long Revolution: Protest Movements and Uprisings* (London: Routledge, 2015), 8.

69 Ibid., 7.

70 Karen Pfeifer, "Economic Reform and Privatization in Egypt," in *The Journey to Tahrir: Revolution, Protest, and Social Change in Egypt*, ed. Jeannie Sowers and Chris Toensing (London: Verso, 2012), 203–222.

71 For more information on the relationship between neoliberalism and the Egyptian uprising, see Angela Joya, "Neoliberalism, the State and Economic Policy Outcomes in the Post-Arab Uprisings: The Case of Egypt," *Mediterranean Politics* 22, no. 3 (2018): 339–361; Bogaert, "Contextualizing the Arab Revolts"; Robert Springborg, "The Precarious Economics of Arab Springs," *Survival: Global Politics and Strategy* 53, no. 6 (2011): 85–104; Ishak Diwan, "Understanding Revolution in the Middle East: The Central Role of the Middle Class," *Middle East Development Journal* 5, no. 1 (2013), doi:10.1142/S1793812013500041.

72 Joya, "Neoliberalism, the State and Economic Policy Outcomes"; Marc Schiffbauer, Sahar Hussain, Hania Sahnoun, and Philip Keefer, *Jobs or Privileges: Unleashing the Employment Potential of the Middle East and North Africa* (2014), https://openknowledge.worldbank.org/handle/10986/20591.

73 See, for instance, the 2006 debate in parliament in which parliamentarians accused government officials of wasting public money over the privatization process of Omar Effendi, a public-owned department store chain: Al-*Ahram* online, "Tahqiqat" [Investigations], www.ahram.org.eg/Archive/2006/6/28/Inve2.html.

74 Sassoon, *Anatomy of Authoritarianism in Arab Republics*.

75 Kandil, *Soldiers, Spies and Statesmen*.

76 Nadine Sika, "Civil Society and Democratization in Egypt: The Road Not Yet Travelled," *Democracy and Society* (Summer 2012): 29–31.

77 For the complete law, see Law No. 84 of the Year 2002 on Non-Governmental Organizations, www.refworld.org/pdfid/5491907d4.pdf (accessed March 2018).

78 Sarah Yerkes, "State-Society Relations after the Arab Spring: New Rulers, Same Rules," *Democracy and Society* (Summer 2012): 9–11.

79 Noha Al Mikawy, *The Building of Consensus in Egypt's Transition Process* (Cairo: AUC Press, 1999).

80 Mona El Ghobashy, "Dynamics of Egypt's Elections," *Middle East Research and Information Project* (September 2010), www.merip.org/mero/mero092910 (accessed June 3, 2018).

81 Paul Schemm, "Activist Dissent and Anti-war Protests in Egypt," in *The Journey to Tahrir: Revolution, Protest and Social Change in Egypt*, ed. Jeannie Sowers and Chris Toensing (London: Verso, 2012), 85–106.

82 Soliman, *Autumn of Dictatorship*, loc3190.

83 Maha Abdelrahman, "A Hierarchy of Struggles? The 'Economic' and 'Political' in Egypt's Revolution," *Review of African Political Economy* 39, no. 134 (2012): 614–628; Abdelrahman, *Egypt's Long Revolution*. See, for instance, Joel Beinin, *Workers and Thieves: Labor Movements and Popular Uprisings in Tunisia and Egypt* (Stanford, CA: Stanford University Press, 2015). See also Joel Beinin, "The Working Class and the Popular Movement in Egypt," in *The Journey to Tahrir: Revolution, Protest, and Social Change in Egypt*, ed. Jeannie Sowers and Chris Toensing (London: Verso, 2012), 92–107.

84 Saloua Ismail, "Urban Subalterns in the Arab Revolutions: Cairo and Damascus in Comparative Perspective," *Comparative Studies in Society and History* 55, no. 4 (2013): 865–894.

85 Amnesty International, "'We Are Not Dirt': Forced Evictions in Egypt's Informal Settlements" (August 23, 2011), www.amnesty.org/download/Documents/32000 /mde12001201ien.pdf (accessed May 17, 2018).

86 Abdelrahman, "Policing Neoliberalism in Egypt."

87 Ibid.

88 Amr Adly, "The Economics of Egypt's Rising Authoritarian System," *Sada: Middle East Analysis* (June 18, 2014), https://carnegieendowment.org/sada /55804.

89 Ibid.

90 See, for instance, Patrick Kingsley, "How Mohamed Morsi, Egypt's First Elected President, Ended up on Death Row," *Guardian*, www.theguardian.com. See also BBC, "Egypt Crisis: Army Ousts President Mohamed Morsi" (July 4, 2013), www .bbc.com/news/world-middle-east-23173794.

91 Amnesty International, "Egypt: Rampant Torture, Arbitrary Arrests and Detentions Signal Catastrophic Decline in Human Rights on Year after Ousting Morsi" (July 3, 2014), www.amnesty.org/en/latest/news/2014/07/egypt-anniver sary-morsi-ousting/.

92 See, for instance, Mohamed Salmawy's article on youth in the 2015 parliamentary elections, and his criticism toward political party leaders in the newspaper *Al Masry Al Youm*, www.almasryalyoum.com/news/details/655123. See also the Minister of Petroleum's comments on the idea that al-Sisi does not need a dominant political party, in *al-Bawaba*, "Wazir al-petrol al-'assbaq fy 'hiwar khas le al-bawaba news" [The former Minister of Petrol in an exclusive interview with al-Bawaba News], www.albawabhnews.com/2360741.

93 Ahmed Morsy, "Egypt's Elections and Parliament: Old Habits Never Die," Tahrir Institute for Middle East Policy (2021), https://timep.org/commentary/analysis /egypts-elections-and-parliament-old-habits-never-die/.

94 International Federation for Human Rights, "Egypt: Elimination of Civil Society Signed into Law by President Sisi" (May 30, 2017), www.fidh.org.
95 Ibid.
96 Ibid.
97 Ibrahim Seif and Ahmed Ghoneim, *The Private Sector in Postrevolutionary Egypt* (Beirut: Carnegie Middle East Center, 2013), 19.
98 Adly, *Economics of Egypt's Rising Authoritarian System.*
99 Robert Springborg, "The Rewards of Failure: Persisting Military Rule in Egypt," *British Journal of Middle Eastern Studies,* https://doi.org/10.1080/13530194.2017.136 3956.
100 Amr Adly, "Economic Recovery in Egypt Won't Guarantee Political Stability," Carnegie Middle East Center (May 20, 2015), http://carnegie-mec.org.
101 World Bank in Egypt, "Overview."
102 Adly, "Economic Recovery."
103 World Bank in Egypt, "Overview."

CHAPTER 2. THE CONSTRUCTION OF YOUTH IN EGYPTIAN POLITICS

1 Mayssoun Sukarieh and Stuart Tannock, "On the Political Economy of Youth: A Comment," *Journal of Youth Studies* 19, no. 9 (2016): 1281–1289, 1282.
2 Brock Bersaglio, Chris Enns, and Thembela Kepe, "Youth under Construction: The United Nations' Representations of Youth in the Global Conversation on the Post-2015 Development Agenda," *Canadian Journal of Development Studies* 36, no. 1 (2015): 57–71, 58.
3 In the Egyptian government's definition, young people are aged eighteen to forty years. See, for instance, Nadine Sika, "Youth Political Engagement in Egypt: From Abstention to Uprising," *British Journal of Middle Eastern Studies* 39, no. 2 (2012): 181–199.
4 Hazem Kandil, *Soldiers, Spies and Statesmen: Egypt's Road to Revolt* (London: Verso, 2012).
5 Joel Gordon, *Nasser's Blessed Movement: Egypt's Free Officers and the July Revolution* (Oxford: Oxford University Press, 1992).
6 See, for instance, Nasser's different speeches to young people on university campuses: www.youtube.com/watch?v=XhYxImyXP50.
7 "Kalimat al-babbasha Jamal abdel Naser fy jami'at al-iskandariya athna' ziarat a'daa majlis qiadat al-thawra laha, 18.4.1953" [Nasser's speech at the University of Alexandria during the visit of the Revolutionary Command Council, April 18, 1953], http://nasser.org/TextViewer.aspx?TextID=SPCH-33-ar (author translation).
8 Laurie Brand, *Official Stories: Politics and National Narratives in Egypt and Algeria* (Stanford, CA: Stanford University Press, 2014); Ahmed Tohamy Abdelhay, *Al-'ajyaal fy al-siyassa al-missriyya dirassat hala l'ijil al-sab'iniyaat* [The generations in Egyptian politics: A case study of the 70s generation] (Cairo: Ahram Center for Strategic Studies, 2009).

9   Kandil, *Soldiers, Spies and Statesmen.*

10 Iliya Harik, "The Single Party as a Subordinate Movement: The Case of Egypt," *World Politics* 26, no. 1 (1973): 80–105.

11 Gordon, *Nasser's Blessed Movement.*

12 Nashaat Edward Adeeb, *Al-thaqafa al-siyassiya l'al-shabab al-jami'yy fy al-mujtama' al-misry* [The political culture of university students in Egyptian society] (Cairo: Al-hay'a al-misriyya al-'ama l'al-kitab, 2009).

13 Gordon, *Nasser's Blessed Movement.*

14 Ibid.

15 Adeeb, *Al-thaqafa al-siyassiya l'al-shabab al-jami'yy fy al-mujtama' al-misry.*

16 Harik, "Single Party as a Subordinate Movement."

17 Steven Cook, *The Struggle for Egypt: From Nasser to Tahrir Square* (Oxford: Oxford University Press, 2011).

18 "Munakashat al-ra'is jamal abdel Nasser wa al-shabab a-lladhin hadaru mu'askar tadrib qiadat al-shabab fy hilwan" [Discussions between president Abdel Nasser and the youth who participated in the youth leadership training camp in Helwan], November 18, 1965, http://nasser.bibalex.org/Data/GR09_1/Speeches/1965/651118_monaqashat.htm (author translation).

19 Abdelhay, *Al-'ajyaal fy al-siyassa al-missriyya dirassat hala l'ijil al-sab'iniyaat.*

20 Ahmed Tohamy, *Youth Activism in Egypt: Islamism, Political Protest and Revolution* (London: I. B. Tauris, 2016).

21 Abdelghafar Shukr, *Al-tali'ya al-'arabiyya: Al-tanzim al-qawmy al-sirry ly jamal-abdel nasser 1965–1986* [The Arab vanguards: The national secret organization of Nasser 1965–1986] (Beirut: Center for Arab Unity Studies, 2015).

22 Cook, *Struggle for Egypt.*

23 Abdelhay, *Al-'ajyaal fy al-siyassa al-missriyya dirassat hala l'ijil al-sab'iniyaat.*

24 Adeeb, *Al-thaqafa al-siyassiya l'al-shabab al-jami'yy fy al-mujtama' al-misry.*

25 Interview with male activist, March 13, 2016.

26 Ibid.

27 Abdelhay, *Al-'ajyaal fy al-siyassa al-missriyya dirassat hala l'ijil al-sab'iniyaat.*

28 Tohamy, *Youth Activism in Egypt.*

29 Ibid.

30 Haggai Erlich, *Students and University in Twentieth Century Egyptian Politics* (London: Frank Cass, 1989); Tohamy, *Youth Activism in Egypt.*

31 Abdelhay, *Al-'ajyaal fy al-siyassa al-missriyya dirassat hala l'ijil al-sab'iniyaat.*

32 Tohamy, *Youth Activism in Egypt.*

33 Adel Abdel Ghafar, *Egyptians in Revolt: The Political Economy of Labor and Student Mobilizations 1919–2011* (London: Routledge, 2017).

34 Ibid.

35 Ibid.

36 Tohamy, *Youth Activism in Egypt*; Ghafar, *Egyptians in Revolt.*

37 Ghafar, *Egyptians in Revolt*, 96–97.

38 Raymond Baker, *Sadat and After: Struggles for Egypt's Political Soul* (Cambridge, MA: Harvard University Press, 1990), 120, cited in Ghafar, *Egyptians in Revolt*, 108.

39 See, for instance, Mayssoun Sukarieh, "From Terrorists to Revolutionaries: The Emergence of 'Youth' in the Arab World and the Discourse of Globalization," *Interface* 4, no. 2 (2012): 424–437; Mayssoun Sukarieh and Stuart Tannock, "In the Best Interests of Youth or Neoliberalism? The World Bank and the New Global Youth Empowerment Project," *Journal of Youth Studies* 11, no. 3 (2008): 301–312; Bersaglio et al., "Youth under Construction."

40 Mayssoun Sukarieh, "On Class, Culture, and the Creation of the Neoliberal Subject: The Case of Jordan," *Anthropological Quarterly* 89, no. 4 (2016): 1201–1225.

41 Nahed Ezz Eddin, "Al-shabab al-'araby wa ru'a al-mustaqbal (Arab Youth and Future Scenarios)," in *Al-shabab al-'araby wa ru'a al-mustaqbal* [Arab youth and the vision for the future] (Beirut: Arab Unity Studies, 2006), 29–98.

42 Abdelhay, *Al-'ajyaal fy al-siyassa al-missriyya dirassat hala l'ijil al-sab'iniyaat*, 21.

43 For more analysis of this wave of contention, see Nadine Sika, *Youth Contentious Politics in Egypt: Dynamics of Continuity and Change* (Cambridge: Cambridge University Press, 2017); Ghafar, *Egyptians in Revolt*.

44 Sika, *Youth Contentious Politics in Egypt*.

45 United Nations Development Programme (UNDP), *Egypt Human Development Report 2010: Youth in Egypt Building Our Future* (Cairo: UNDP, 2010).

46 Dina Shehata, *'Audat al-siyassa* [The return of politics] (Cairo: Ahram Center for Political and Strategic Studies, 2010); Sika, *Youth Contentious Politics in Egypt*.

47 Maha Abdelrahman, *Egypt's Long Revolution: Protest Movements and Uprisings* (London: Routledge, 2015); Sika, *Youth Contentious Politics in Egypt*.

48 UNDP, *Egypt Human Development Report 2010*, viii.

49 Focus group, April 2015.

50 Ibid.

51 Rania Roushdy and Maia Sieverding, *Panel Survey of Young People in Egypt 2014: Generating Evidence for Policy* (Cairo: Population Council, 2015).

52 Erica Frantz and Andrea Kendall-Taylor, "A Dictator's Toolkit: Understanding How Co-optation Affects Repression in Autocracies," *Journal of Peace Research* 51, no. 3 (2014): 332–346; Ronald Wintrobe, *The Political Economy of Dictatorship* (Cambridge: Cambridge University Press, 1998); Barbara Geddes, *Paradigms and Sand Castles* (Ann Arbor: University of Michigan Press, 2003).

53 Beatriz Magaloni, "Credible Power-Sharing and the Longevity of Authoritarian Rule," *Comparative Political Studies* 41, no. 4–5 (2008): 715–741.

54 Sika, "Youth Political Engagement in Egypt."

55 Mohammed Zahid, "The Egyptian Nexus: The Rise of Gamal Mubarak, the Politics of Succession and the Challenges of the Muslim Brotherhood," *Journal of North African Studies* 15, no. 2 (2010): 217–230.

56 Focus group, May 2, 2015.

57 Abdelhay, *Al-'ajyaal fy al-siyassa al-missriyya dirassat hala l'ijil al-sab'iniyaat*, 27.

58 Sika, "Youth Political Engagement in Egypt."

59 Abdelhay, *Al-'ajyaal fy al-siyassa al-missriyya dirassat hala l'ijil al-sab'iniyaat*.

60 Ghafar, *Egyptians in Revolt*.

61 Abdelrahman, *Egypt's Long Revolution*, 92.

62 For more information on this incident, see "Egyptian 'Battle of the Camels' Officials Acquitted," *BBC* (October 10, 2012), www.bbc.com/news/world-middle-east-19905435.

63 See YouTube, "Activists Chants" (February 11, 2011), www.youtube.com/watch?v=2Kpgf6Jqkfk (accessed October 24, 2015).

64 See, for instance, "Text of Omar Suleiman's Address," *New York Times*, February 11, 2011, www.nytimes.com (accessed March 28, 2018).

65 Ibid.

66 Salma Shukrallah, "Once Election Allies, Egypt's 'Fairmont' Opposition Turn against Morsi," *Al-Ahram* (June 27, 2013), http://english.ahram.org.eg (accessed May 2, 2018).

67 Sika, *Youth Contentious Politics in Egypt*.

68 Ahmed Abd Rabou, "Al-jami'a wa al-siyassa" [University and politics], *Almalaf al-misry* (2014): 5–7; see also Ahmed Abd Rabou, "The Institutionalization of Academic Freedom Violations in Egypt," *Al-Fanar Media*, July 3, 2015, www.al-fanarmedia.org/2015/07/the-institutionalization-of-academic-freedom-violations-in-egypt/.

69 See, for instance, "Al-mahrassawy yakshif haqiqat 'audet intikhabat itihad tolaab jame'at al-azhar" [Al-mahrassawy discusses the truth behind the return of the student union elections in al-Azhar university], www.albawabhnews.com/3784936 (accessed December 26, 2019).

70 Interview with former al-Azhar university student union member, July 11, 2015.

71 Mostafa Hashem Youssef, "Government, Brotherhood Fail to Attract Egyptian Youth," *Al-Monitor* (January 29, 2014).

72 Michelle Dunne and Katie Bentivoglio, "Student Protests: The Beginning or the End of Youth Dissent?" Carnegie Middle East Center (2014), http://carnegie-mec.org/diwan/56984?lang=en (accessed May 5, 2018).

73 Ibid.

74 Ibid.

75 Nagah Hussein, "The Crisis of Egypt's Youth," *Fikra Forum* (December 1, 2014), http://fikraforum.org/?p=6153#.VohiBFdIpE4.

76 Dunne and Bentivoglio, "Student Protests."

77 Azzurra Meringolo, "The Struggle over the Egyptian Public Sphere," *Istituto Affari Internazionali Working Papers*, no. 15/4 (Rome: IAI, 2015), www.iai.it/sites/default/files/iaiwp1504.pdf.

78 Ibid.

79 For more information on the human rights status in Egypt, see Freedom House, "Freedom in the World: Egypt 2015," https://freedomhouse.org/report/freedom -world/2015/egypt#.VWiKEWRViko.

80 For more information on the protest law, see JURIST, "Egypt's New Cybercrime Law: Another Legislative Failure," www.jurist.org/forum/2016/07/mohamed -abdelaal-egypt-cybercrime.php. See also Dunne and Bentivoglio, "Student Protests."

81 Thanassis Cambanis, "Is Egypt on the Verge of Another Uprising?," *Atlantic* (January 16, 2015), www.theatlantic.com (accessed May 6, 2018).

82 Ahmed Ezzat, *You Are Being Watched! Egypt's Mass Internet Surveillance* (September 29, 2014), www.madamasr.com/opinion/politics/you-are-being -watched-egypts-mass-internet-surveillance (accessed May 6, 2018).

83 Following President al-Sisi's remarks at the Arab Summit held at the end of March 2015 at Sharm el-Sheikh, and in a conversation with Sam Kutesa, president of the UN General Assembly.

84 Ezzat, *You Are Being Watched!*

85 Ragab Saad, "Egypt's Draft Cybercrime Law Undermines Freedom of Expression" (April 25, 2015), www.atlanticcouncil.org/blogs/menasource/egypt-s-draft-cyber crime-law-undermines-freedom-of-expression/ (accessed May 8, 2018).

86 Ibid.

87 For more information on the number of dead and injured and for a detailed description of this affair, see Human Rights Watch, "All According to Plan: The Rab'a Massacre and Mass Killings of Protesters in Egypt," www.hrw.org/report /2014/08/12/all-according-plan/raba-massacre-and-mass-killings-protesters -egypt.

88 Hatem Zayed, Nadine Sika, and Ibrahim Elnur, "The Student Movement in Egypt: A Microcosm of Contentious Politics" (September 19, 2016), www.iai.it/sites /default/files/p2y_19.pdf.

89 Presidential Leadership Programme, *Al-birnamej al-ri'assy le ta'hiil al-shabab l'al-qiada* [Presidential Leadership Programme for preparing youth for leadership] (2015), https://plp.eg/en/about-plp/ (accessed May 8, 2018).

90 Interview with former instructor at the Presidential Leadership Programme, April 4, 2018.

91 See, for instance, the last conference that was held in November 2017 under al-Sisi's auspices, on the World Youth Forum's website, https://egyouth.com/en/.

92 Focus group, May 2, 2015.

CHAPTER 3. DILEMMAS OF CIVIC AND POLITICAL ENGAGEMENT

1 Albert Hirschman, *Exit, Voice, and Loyalty: Responses to Decline in Firms, Organizations and States* (Cambridge, MA: Harvard University Press, 1970).

2 For more analysis on the distinction between how citizens perceive the regime, and act in compliance to its power, while not necessarily perceiving the regime to

be a legitimate actor, see Lisa Wedeen, *Authoritarian Apprehensions: Ideology, Judgement and Mourning in Syria* (Chicago: University of Chicago Press, 2019).

3 Population Council, *Survey of Young People in Egypt: 2011* (2011), www.popcoun cil.org/uploads/pdfs/2010PGY_SYPEFinalReport.pdf, p. 135.

4 For more information on the qualitative fieldwork, see the introduction. For more information on the survey methodology, see http://power2youth.iai.it/survey .html.

5 Guillermo O'Donnell, Philippe Schmitter, and Laurence Whitehead, *Transitions from Authoritarian Rule: Comparative Perspectives* (Baltimore, MD: Johns Hopkins University Press, 1986); Rex Brynen, Bahgat Korany, and Paul Noble, *Political Liberalization and Democratization in the Arab World: Vol. 1 Theoretical Perspectives* (Boulder, CO: Lynne Rienner, 1995); Augustus R. Norton, "The Future of Civil Society in the Middle East," *Middle East Journal* 47, no. 1 (1993): 205–216.

6 Eberhard Kienle, "Democracy Promotion and the Renewal of Authoritarian Rule," in *Debating Arab Authoritarianism: Dynamics and Durability in Nondemocratic Regimes*, ed. Oliver Schlumberger (Stanford, CA: Stanford University Press, 2007), 231–250; Oliver Schlumberger, *Debating Arab Authoritarianism: Dynamics and Durability in Nondemocratic Regimes* (Stanford, CA: Stanford University Press, 2007); Sheila Carapico, *Political Aid and Arab Activism* (Cambridge: Cambridge University Press, 2014); Vicki Langhor, "Too Much Civil Society, Too Little Politics: Egypt and Liberalizing Arab Regimes," *Comparative Politics* 36, no. 2 (2004): 181–204.

7 Christopher Heulin, "Governing Civil Society: The Political Logic of NGO-State Relations Under Dictatorships," *Voluntas* (2009): 220–239.

8 Toby Carroll and Darryl S. L. Jarvis, "The New Politics of Development: Citizens, Civil Society, and the Evolution of Neoliberal Development Policy," *Globalizations* 12, no. 3 (2015): 281–304.

9 Ibid., 284.

10 Ibid.

11 Ibid.

12 Mohamed al-Agaty, "Qira'a fy qanun al-jam'iyyat al-ahliyya: Ijhad jadid ly al-isslah" [A reading of the NGO law: Another termination of reform], *Majalet al-dimuqratiyya* [Democracy journal] 65 (2016), http://democracy.ahram.org.eg.

13 Francesco Cavatrota and Vincent Durac, *Civil Society and Democratization in the Arab World: The Dynamics of Activism* (New York: Routledge, 2011).

14 Mohamed al-Agaty, *Al tamweel al-ajnaby le'al mujtama' al-madani fy misr ba'd thawrat 25 yanayir: Al-waqe' wa al-tahadiyyat wa al-ma'ayeer* [Foreign funding for NGOs in Egypt in the aftermath of the January 25 revolution: Reality, challenges and benchmarks], Arab Forum for Alternatives Working Papers, www.afaleba non.org/ar/publication/5529/. See chapter 1 for more details on this law.

15 al-Agaty, "Qira'a fy qanun al-jam'iyyat al-ahliyya."

16 For more information on this initiative, see "Ta'araf 'ala injazaat mubadaret 'fekretak sherketak'mundh intelaqeha 'am 2017" [Get to know the main accomplishments of the "your idea, your company" initiative since its establishment in 2017] (July 14, 2021), Akhbar al-youm.

17 Population Council, *Survey of Young People in Egypt: 2011*, 135.

18 Nadine Sika, Hatem Fayez, Rana Gaber, Batoul al Mehdar, and Alia Alaa Eddin, "Mapping of Civil Society Organizations and Political Parties in Egypt after the Arab Uprisings" (2015), unpublished report for the P2Y project, on file with the author.

19 Dina Shehata, "Youth Movements and the 25 January Revolution," in *Arab Spring in Egypt: Revolution and Beyond*, ed. Bahgat Korany and Rabab El-Mahdi (Cairo: American University in Cairo Press, 2012), 327–351; Nadine Sika, "Dynamics of a Stagnant Religious Discourse and the Rise of New Secular Movements in Egypt," in Korany and El-Mahdi, *Arab Spring in Egypt*, 63–80; Frederic Vairel, "Protesting in Authoritarian Situations: Egypt and Morocco in Comparative Perspective," in *Movements, Mobilization, and Contestation in the Middle East and North Africa*, ed. Joel Beinin and Frederic Vairel (Stanford, CA: Stanford University Press, 2013), 33–48.

20 Interview, August 2015.

21 *Al-Ahram*, "Parliamentary Elections" (October 16, 2015), www.ahram.org.eg /News/131694/145/443978/ (accessed May 7, 2018).

22 Al Youm 7, " 'Hansharek' . . . hamla l'ehath al-shabab 'ala al-musharaka fy al-initikhabat wa da'am al-sisi" ["We will Participate" a campaign to urge young people to participate in elections and support al-Sisi] (March 4, 2018), www .youm7.com.

23 Mayssoun Sukarieh and Stuart Tannock, "The Positivity Imperative: A Critical Look at the 'New' Youth Development Movement," *Journal of Youth Studies* 14, no. 6 (2011): 675–691.

24 See, for instance, the debate concerning the role of the World Bank in promoting this discourse on youth, in Mayssoun Sukarieh and Stuart Tannock, "In the Best Interest of Youth or Neoliberalism? The World Bank and the New Global Youth Empowerment Project," *Journal of Youth Studies* 11, no. 3 (2008): 301–312.

25 Interview, August 2015.

26 Focus group, May 2015.

27 Ibid.

28 See, for instance, the case of the clampdown against *Mada Masr* and its staff in 2019. *Guardian*, "Egypt's Security Forces Raid Online Newspaper's Office in Cairo," www.theguardian.com (accessed November 25, 2019).

29 This was discussed at length during the focus groups.

30 Interview, July 2015.

31 Interview, August 2015.

32 June 13 was when a coup was attempted against then-president Mohamed Morsi.

33 Interview, August 2015.
34 Interview, September 2015.
35 Interview, August 2015.
36 Ibid.
37 Lisa Richey and Stefano Ponte, "New Actors and Alliances in Development," *Third World Quarterly* 35, no. 1 (2014): 1–21.
38 Linsey McGoey, "The Philanthropic State: Market-State Hybrids in the Philanthrocapitalist Turn," *Third World Quarterly* 35, no. 1 (2014): 109–125.
39 Charles Harvey, Mairi Maclean, and Roy Suddaby, "Historical Perspectives on Entrepreneurship and Philanthropy," *Business History Review* 93 (Autumn 2019): 443–471.
40 Focus group, May 2015.
41 Ibid.
42 Ibid.
43 Ibid.
44 Focus group, April 2015.
45 Focus group, May 2015.
46 Focus group, April 2015; focus group, May 2015.
47 Interview, July 2015.
48 Focus group, May 2015.
49 Ibid.
50 The al-Dostour Party (or Constitution Party) is an opposition political party that was established by Nobel Peace laureate Mohamed El Baradei in 2012.
51 Focus group, May 2015.
52 The Free Egyptians' Party is liberal and close to the ruling elite; it was also established by a prominent Egyptian businessman. The Mostaqbal Watan Party is believed to have been established by the state security apparatus to co-opt young people.
53 Focus group, May 2015.
54 Reuters, "Pro-Sisi Party Wins Majority in Egypt's Parliamentary Polls" (December 14, 2020), www.reuters.com. For more analysis on how this political party is moving toward a dominant political party, see Dina Shehata, "The Senate and the Return of Party Politics," Al-*Ahram* (October 29, 2020), http://english.ahram.org.eg.
55 Jason Brownlee, *Authoritarianism in an Age of Democracy* (Cambridge: Cambridge University Press, 2007).
56 See, for instance, Ibrahim Ismail Abdu Mohamed, "Al-tahawulaat al-ijtima'iyya ma ba'd al-rabi' al-'araby wa in'ikassateha 'ala al-shabab min manzur al-ijtima' al-siyassy: Dirassat halat misr min khilal al-fatra min 2011–2018" [Post–Arab Spring social transformations and their repercussions on youth from a political sociology perspective: A case study of Egypt from 2011–2018], Jil Scientific Research Center, http://jilrc.com.

See also Howaida Roman, "Al-tabaqa al-wusta fy misr: Ta'hawulat wa ta'hadiyat" [The middle class in Egypt: Developments and challenges], *Majalet al-dimuqratiyya* (2018), https://seketmaaref.files.wordpress.com/2018/04/d985d8a cd984d8a9-d8a7d984d8afd98ad985d982d8b1d8a7d8b7d98ad8a9-d8a7d984d8b 7d8a8d982d8a9-d8a7d984d988d8b3d8b7d989-d981d989-d985d8b5d8b1.pdf.

57 Victoria Bernal and Inderpal Grewal, "The NGO Form: Feminist Struggles, States and Neoliberalism," in *Theorising NGOs: States, Feminists, and Neoliberalism,* ed. Victoria Bernal and Inderpal Grewal (Durham, NC: Duke University Press, 2014), 1–18.

58 Mervat Hatem, "First Ladies and the (Re)Definition of the Authoritarian State in Egypt," *POMEPS Studies* 19 (2016): 42–44.

59 Interview, November 2015.

60 Interview, July 2015.

61 Ibid.

62 Interview, August 2015.

63 See, for instance, *Al Watan News'* account of al-Sisi's acceptance of the virginity tests, www.youtube.com/watch?v=o4dcC4nLUmE

64 Ghada Ghalib, "CNN: Kushuf al-'uthriyya tahdaf ila idhlal wa irhab al-mutazaherat al-missriyat" [CNN: Virginity tests promote a climate of fear among female Egyptian protesters], *Al-Masry al Youm* (February 22, 2014).

65 "Egyptian MP Calls for Mandatory Virginity Tests for Admittance of Women to University," *Egyptian Streets* (September 30, 2016), https://egyptianstreets.com (accessed May 7, 2018).

66 Sarah Sirgany, "Outcry in Egypt after Lawmaker Proposes 'Virginity Tests' University Entry," *CNN* (2016), https://edition.cnn.com.

67 Ruba Salih, Lynn Welchman, and Elena Zambelli, "Gender, Intersectionality and Youth Civic and Political Engagement: An Analysis of the Meso Level Factors of Youth Exclusion/Inclusion in the South and East Mediterranean (SEM) Region," Power2Youth working paper no. 24 (February 2017), 5.

68 For more discussions on patriarchy and women quotas, see Lindsay Benstead, "Conceptualizing and Measuring Patriarchy: The Importance of Feminist Theory," *Mediterranean Politics* (2020), doi:10.1080/13629395.2020.1729627. See also Marwa Shalaby and Laila Elimam, "Women in Legislative Committees in Arab Parliaments," *Comparative Politics* 53, no. 1 (2020): 139–167.

69 These include both the hope and the threat.

70 Focus group, April 2015; focus group, May 2015.

71 Interview, July 2015.

72 Interview, November 2015.

73 Interview, August 2015.

74 Interview, May 2015.

75 Interview, June 2015.

76 Brock Bersaglio, Chris Enns, and Thembela Kepe, "Youth under Construction: The United Nations' Representations of Youth in the Global Conversation on the Post-2015 Development Agenda," *Canadian Journal of Development Studies* 36, no. 1 (2015): 57–71.

CHAPTER 4. YOUNG POLITICAL ACTIVISTS

1 See, for instance, Dina Shehata, *Audat al-siyassa* [The return of politics] (Cairo: Al Ahram Center for Political and Strategic Studies, 2010); Nadine Sika, *Youth Activism and Contentious Politics in Egypt: Dynamics of Continuity and Change* (Cambridge: Cambridge University Press, 2017); Rabab El Mahdi, "Enough! Egypt's Quest for Democracy," *Comparative Political Studies* 42, no. 8 (2009): 1011–1039.

2 Jason Brownlee, Tarek Masoud, and Andrew Reynolds, *The Arab Spring: Pathways of Repression and Reform* (Oxford: Oxford University Press, 2015), 72.

3 Ibid., 75.

4 For more accounts on relations between the army and Brotherhood during the interim period, see Zeinab Abul-Magd, "Egypt's Adaptable Officers: Business, Nationalism and Discontent," in *Businessmen in Arms: The Military and Other Armed Groups Profit in the MENA Region*, ed. Elke Gerwart and Zeinab Abul-Magd (Lanham, MD: Rowman and Littlefield, 2016), 23–42.

5 Ibid.

6 Ibid.

7 Milan Svolik, *The Politics of Authoritarian Rule* (New York: Cambridge University Press, 2012).

8 Abul-Magd, "Egypt's Adaptable Officers."

9 Carl Friedrich and Zbigniew Brzezinski, *Totalitarian Dictatorship* (Cambridge, MA: Harvard University Press, 1965).

10 Daniela Stockmann and Mary Gallagher, "Remote Control: How the Media Sustain Authoritarian Rule in China," *Comparative Political Studies* 44, no. 4 (2011): 436–467.

11 Barbara Geddes and John Zaller, "Sources of Popular Support for Authoritarian Regimes," *American Journal of Political Science* 33, no. 2 (1989): 319–347.

12 Elizabeth A. Stein, "The Unraveling of Support for Authoritarianism: The Dynamic Relationship of Media, Elites, and Public Opinion in Brazil, 1972–82," *International Journal of Press/Politics* 18, no. 1 (2013): 85–107.

13 Espen Geelmuyden Rød, "Empowering Activists or Autocrats? The Internet in Authoritarian Regimes," *Journal of Peace Research* 52, no. 3 (2015): 338–351.

14 For more discussions of these different authoritarian survival strategies, see Sika, *Youth Activism and Contentious Politics in Egypt.*

15 Steven Heydemann and Reinoud Leenders, "Authoritarian Learning and Counterrevolution," in *The Arab Uprisings Explained: New Contentious Politics in*

the Middle East, ed. Marc Lynch (New York: Columbia University Press, 2014), 75–92.

16 Johannes Gerschewski, "The Three Pillars of Stability: Legitimation, Repression, and Cooptation in Autocratic Regimes," *Democratization* 20, no. 1 (2013): 13–38; Christian Davenport, "State Repression and Political Order," *Annual Review of Political Science* 101, no. 1 (2007): 1–23; Christian Davenport, "Regimes, Repertoires and State Repression," *Swiss Political Science Review* 15, no. 2 (2009): 377–385.

17 Davenport, "State Repression and Political Order."

18 Davenport, "Regimes, Repertoires and State Repression."

19 Arne Roets, Ilse Cornelis, and Alain van Hiel, "Openness as a Predictor of Political Orientation and Conventional and Unconventional Political Activism in Western and Eastern Europe," *Journal of Personality Assessment* 92, no. 1 (2014): 53–63.

20 Ibid.

21 The activists under analysis in the chapter are members of the following parties and movements: April 6 Youth Movement, Muslim Brotherhood, Ultras Ahlawy and Ulras White Knights, the former Freedom and Justice Party (FJP), Masr al-Horeya, Masr al-Qaweya, al-Wasat, al-Tahalof al-Shaaby, al-Dostour, Egyptian Initiative for Personal Rights (EIPR), Association for Freedom of Thought and Expression (AFTE), and Morsy Meter.

22 For more discussion on co-optation and fragmentation, see Nadine Sika, "Repression, Co-optation and Movement Fragmentation: Evidence from the Youth Movement in Egypt," *Political Studies* 67, no. 3 (2019): 676–692.

23 Interview, September 2015.

24 Interview, September 2015. By "his own people," the interviewee refers to young people from high socioeconomic sectors. The "selfie" reference was about the president's selfie with young ushers during the Sharm El Sheikh Economic summit, which went viral in the formal and informal media outlets in Egypt.

25 Focus group, May 2015.

26 Interview, September 2015.

27 Interview, August 2015.

28 For more discussions on regime co-optation strategies and their impact on youth movements' fragmentation, see Sika, "Repression, Co-optation, and Movement Fragmentation."

29 Stockmann and Gallagher, "Remote Control."

30 Interview, August 2015.

31 Ibid.

32 Stein, "Unraveling of Support for Authoritarianism."

33 Dina Bishara, "The Politics of Ignoring: Protest Dynamics in Late Mubarak Egypt," *Perspectives on Politics* 13, no. 4 (2015): 958–975.

34 Neil Ketchley, *Egypt in a Time of Revolution: Contentious Politics and the Arab Spring* (Cambridge: Cambridge University Press, 2017); Jannis Grimm and Cilja

Harders, "Unpacking the Effects of Repression: The Evolution of Islamists' Repertoires of Contention in Egypt after the Fall of President Morsi," *Social Movement Studies* 17, no. 1 (2018): 1–18.

35 Joshua Stacher, "Fragmenting States, New Regimes: Militarized State Violence and Transition in the Middle East," *Democratization* 22, no. 2 (2015): 259–275.

36 Grimm and Harders, "Unpacking the Effects of Repression."

37 Rabab El Mahdi, "The Failure of the Regime or the Demise of the State?," *International Journal of Middle East Studies* 50, no. 2 (2018): 328–332.

38 For more accounts on the regime's strategies during these events, see *Middle East Eye*, "The Rabaa Massacre and Egyptian Propaganda," www.middleeasteye.net. See also Grimm and Harders, "Unpacking the Effects of Repression."

39 Maha Abdelrahman, "Policing Neoliberalism in Egypt: The Continuing Rise of the 'Securocratic' State," *Third World Quarterly* 38, no. 1 (2017): 185–202, 193.

40 Interview, October 14, 2015.

41 Khalil al-Anani, "Rethinking the Repression-Dissent Nexus: Assessing Egypt's Muslim Brotherhood's Response to Repression since the Coup of 2013," *Democratization* 26, no. 8 (2019): 1329–1341, 1334.

42 Ibid.

43 Interview, August 2015.

44 Ibid.

45 Ibid.

46 Ibid.

47 Interview, September 2015.

48 Ibid.

49 Interview, May 2015.

50 For more information on these events, see BBC, "Egypt: The Legacy of Mohamed Mahmoud Street," www.bbc.com (accessed July 20, 2017).

51 Focus group, May 2015.

52 Focus group, April 2015.

53 Focus group, May 2015.

54 Ibid.

55 Interview, September 2015.

56 Jan Jämte and Rune Ellefsen, "The Consequences of Soft Repression," *Mobilization: An International Journal* 25, no. 3 (2020): 383–404.

57 Interview, May 2015.

58 Focus group, May 2015.

59 Interview, July 2015.

60 For more information on violence in Port Said, see BBC, "Tassalssol zamany le qadiyyet majzaret port-said" [The timeline of the Port-Said massacre], www.bbc.com.

61 Focus group, May 2015.

62 Interview, August 2015.

63 Ibid.

64 Interview, September 2015.

65 al-Anani, "Rethinking the Repression-Dissent Nexus," 1337.

66 Ibid.

67 For more information on Injaz, see http://injaz-egypt.org/.

68 Interview, June 2015.

69 Interview, August 2015.

70 Focus group, May 2015.

71 Ali Hourani, "From 'the Effect of Repression' toward 'the Response to Repression,'" *Current Sociology Review* 66, no. 6 (2018): 950–973.

72 For more discussions on this, see Andrea Teti et al., *Democratisation against Democracy: How EU Foreign Policy Fails the Middle East* (London: Palgrave Macmillan, 2020).

73 Asef Bayat, *Revolution without Revolutionaries* (Stanford, CA: Stanford University Press, 2018), 158.

74 Ibid.

75 Interview, July 2015.

76 Interview, August 2015.

77 Interview, September 2015.

78 Interview, July 2015.

79 Interview, September 2015; focus group, April 2015.

80 Interview, September 2015.

81 Ibid.

82 Ibid.

83 Abdelrahman, "Policing Neoliberalism in Egypt."

84 Interview, August 2015.

CHAPTER 5. YOUTH POVERTY

1 Mona Abaza, "Violence, Dramaturgical Repertoires and Neoliberal Imaginaries in Cairo," *Theory Culture and Society* 33, no. 7–8 (2016): 111–135.

2 Fatima Ramadan and Amr Adly, *Low-Cost Authoritarianism: The Egyptian Regime and the Labor Movement since 2013* (Washington, DC: Carnegie Endowment for International Peace, 2015).

3 Abaza, "Violence."

4 Ahmed Bahaa Eddin Shaaban, *Sira' al-tabakat fy misr al-mu'assara: Mukademat thawrat 25 yanayer 2011* [Class conflict in Egypt: Preparations for 25 January 2011 revolution] (Cairo: Maktabet al-ussra, 2012).

5 Assefa Merete, Bruce Piozzi, and Laurence M. Sommers, "Concepts in Social and Spatial Marginality," *Geografiska Annaler. Series B, Human Geography* 82, no. 2 (2000): 89–101.

6 Christopher C. Ntombi, "Globalization and the Threat of Marginalization," *SSRN Electronic Journal* (August 2009), doi:10.2139/ssrn.1446864.

7   Guy Standing, "The Precariat: Today's Transformative Class?," *Development* 61 (2018): 115–121.

8   Ibid., 117.

9   Maria Cristina Paciello and Daniela Pioppi, "Working Class Youth Transitions as a Litmus Test for Change: Labour Crisis and Social Conflict in Arab Mediterranean Countries," *Mediterranean Politics*, doi:10.1080/13629395.2020 .1749814.

10 Paciello and Pioppi, "Working Class Youth Transitions," 1. See also Robert MacDonald, "Youth Transitions, Unemployment and Underemployment: Plus ça change, plus c'est la même chose?," *Journal of Sociology* 47, no. 4 (2011): 427–444.

11 Interview, November 2015.

12 Saloua Ismail, "Urban Subalterns in the Arab Revolutions: Cairo and Damascus in Comparative Perspective," *Comparative Studies in Society and History* 55, no. 4 (2013): 865–894, 872.

13 Abdel-Rahman Hussein, "Was the Egyptian Revolution Really Non-violent?," *Egypt Independent* (January 24, 2012), www.egyptindependent.com (accessed May 17, 2018).

14 Joel Beinin, "The Working Class and the Popular Movement in Egypt," in *The Journey to Tahrir: Revolution, Protest, and Social Change in Egypt*, ed. Jeannie Sowers and Chris Toensing (London: Verso, 2012), 92–107.

15 Amnesty International, "'We Are Not Dirt': Forced Evictions in Egypt's Informal Settlements" (August 23, 2011), www.amnesty.org (accessed May 17, 2018).

16 Egyptian Center for Economic Studies (ECES), *Egypt's Economic Profile and Statistics* (Cairo: ECES, 2018), 25. In 2010 one US dollar was at 5.74 Egyptian pounds. In 2017 one US dollar was 17.7 Egyptian pounds.

17 Calyd T. Cerio, "Revisiting the Sociological Theories of Poverty: Conceptualizing a Framework for Rural Poverty in the Philippines," *Transatlantic Journal of Rural Research* 1, no. 1 (2019): 34–52.

18 Ibid., 35.

19 Harry Pettit, " 'Iftar' in McDonald's: The Everyday Encroachment of Cairo's Subaltern Cosmopolitans," in *Contentious Politics in the Middle East: Popular Resistance and Marginalized Activism beyond the Arab Uprisings*, ed. Fawaz Gerges (New York: Palgrave Macmillan, 2015), 523–546.

20 Filipe R. Companate and Davin Chor, "Why Was the Arab World Poised for Revolution? Schooling, Economic Opportunities, and the Arab Spring," *Journal of Economic Perspectives* 26, no. 2 (2012): 167–188.

21 Interview, July 2015.

22 Interview, August 2015.

23 Focus group, May 2015.

24 Focus group, April 2015.

25 Interview, June 2015.

26 Interview, August 2015.

27 This young man was not one of the five young people living in informal settlements and Upper Egypt. He was a student from a middle-income family living in
Cairo that could not afford a private university, yet he had been awarded a
scholarship to study there.

28 Interview, July 2015.

29 Interview, September 2015. The income was less than 3,000 EGP (Egyptian
pounds). In 2015 this was US$300; in 2018 this amounts to US$169 per month.

30 Ibid.

31 Interview, November 2015.

32 Ray Bush, "Poverty and Neo-liberal Bias in the Middle East and North Africa,"
Development and Change 35, no. 4 (2004): 673–695.

33 Koenraad Bogaert, "Contextualizing the Arab Revolts: The Politics behind Three
Decades of Neoliberalism in the Arab World," *Middle East Critique* 22, no. 3
(2013): 213–234.

34 Mohamed Soliman, "Egypt's Informal Economy: An Ongoing Cause of Unrest,"
Journal of International Affairs 73, no. 2 (Spring/Summer 2020): 185–194.

35 This section is largely dependent on Nadine Sika, "Neolberalism, Marginalization
and the Uncertainties of Being Young: The Case of Egypt," *Mediterranean Politics*,
vol. 24, no. 19 (2019): 545–567; Magued Osman, "Al-'adala wa al-insaf fy iltihaaq
al-sharai'h al-mukhtalifa bi al-ta'lim al-jami'y" [Socioeconomic equity in
university education in Egypt] (2015), www. popcouncil.org/uploads/pdfs/2015
PGY_SocioEconomicEquityEgypt_ar.pdf.

36 European Training Foundation, "Youth in Transition in the Southern and Eastern
Mediterranean: Identifying Profiles and Characteristics to Tap into Young People's
Potential with Case Studies on Egypt and Jordan" (2021), www.etf.europa.eu/sites
/default/files/2021-03/youth_in_semed.pdf, p. 39.

37 Ragui Assaad and Ghada Barsoum, "Youth Exclusion in Egypt: In Search of
'Second Chances,'" Middle East Youth Initiative working paper (September 2007),
http://dataopics.worldbank.org/hnp/files/edstats/EGYpub07.pdf; Ragui Assaad
and Caroline Krafft, *The Structure and Evolution of Employment in Egypt:
1998–2012* (Cairo: Economic Research Forum, 2013).

38 Ahmed Ghoneim, "Evaluating the Institutional Framework Governing Migration
in Egypt," in *Partners in Development Conference: Irregular Migration* (Cairo:
Partners in Development, 2009).

39 Edward Sayre, "Labor Force Conditions of the Middle East Youth," in *Political and
Socio-economic changes in the Middle East and North Africa: Gender Perspectives
and Survival Strategies*, ed. Roksana Bahramitash and Hadi Salehi Esfahani
(London: Palgrave Macmillan, 2016), 75–98.

40 For more information on the quantitative and qualitative data, refer to chapter 3.

41 See, for instance, Ragui Assad, Rana Hendy, Moundir Lassassi, and Shaimaa
Yassin, "Explaining the MENA Paradox: Rising Educational Attainment, Yet
Stagnant Female Labor Force Participation," IZA Institute of Labor Economics

Discussion Paper Series, no. 11385 (2018), http://ftp.iza.org/dp11385.pdf (accessed December 30, 2019). See also Ragui Assad and Caroline Krafft, "Labor Market Dynamics and Youth Unemployment in the Middle East and North Africa: Evidence from Egypt, Jordan and Tunisia," Economic Research Forum Working Paper Series No. 993 (2016).

42 See tables 5.2 and 5.3.

43 For more discussions on this, see Nadine Sika, "Neoliberalism, Marginalization and the Uncertainties of Being Young," *Mediterranean Politics* 24, no. 5 (2019): 545–567.

44 Interview, May 2015.

45 Interview, September 2015.

46 Interview, November 2015.

47 Interview, September 2015.

48 See, for instance, the discussion in Amr Adly, *Cleft Capitalism: The Social Origins of Failed Market Making in Egypt* (Stanford, CA: Stanford University Press, 2020), concerning the root causes of unemployment, which depend more on the structure of the cleft capitalist system than on cronyism and corruption per se. See also Angela Joya, *The Roots of Revolt: A Political Economy of Egypt from Nasser to Mubarak* (Cambridge: Cambridge University Press, 2020).

49 Transparency International, "The Alarming Message of Egypt's Constitutional Amendments" (February 13, 2019), www.transparency.org.

50 Standing, "Precariat."

51 This amounts to almost US$100–300, at the exchange value between US dollars and Egyptian pounds in April 2016 when the survey was implemented. In 2017, the exchange rate is at US$50–150 after the devaluation of the Egyptian pound in November 2016.

52 Joya, *Roots of Revolt*, 173.

53 Ibid.

54 Bush, "Poverty and Neo-liberal Bias."

55 Paciello and Pioppi, "Working Class Youth Transitions."

56 Interview, August 2015.

57 For more discussions on youth unemployment, underemployment, and uncertainties, see Jörg Gertel and Ralf Hexel, eds., *Coping with Uncertainty: Youth in the Middle East and North Africa* (London: Saqi, 2018).

58 See *Mada Masr*, "Al-ta'bi'a wa al-ihsaa: 915 junayhan mutawasset al-ajr al-'usbu'iyy al-'am al-mady" [Central Agency for Public Mobilization and Statistics: 915 Egyptian pounds (EGP) average weekly income last year] (August 20, 2021), www .madamasr.com.

59 See, for instance, Michael Hoffman and Amaney Jamal, "The Youth and the Arab Spring: Cohort Differences and Similarities," *Middle East Law and Governance* 4 (2012): 168–188. See also Gertel and Hexel, *Coping with Uncertainty*.

60 See, for instance, Lisa Blaydes, *Elections and Distributive Politics in Mubarak's Egypt* (New York: Cambridge University Press, 2011); and Jennifer Gandhi and

Ellen Lust, "Elections under Authoritarianism," *Annual Review of Political Science* 12 (2009): 403–422.

61 See tables 3.1 and 3.2.

62 See table 3.3.

63 See chapter 3 for more discussion about the denial of permissions for questions on protest activities.

64 Carina Mood and Jan Jonsson, "The Social Consequences of Poverty: An Empirical Test on Longitudinal Data," *Social Indicators Research* 127 (2016): 633–652.

65 Claudio Holzner, "The Poverty of Democracy: Neoliberal Reforms and Political Participation of the Poor in Mexico," *Latin American Politics and Society* 49, no. 2 (2007): 87–122, 91.

66 Diane Singerman, *Avenues of Participation: Family, Politics and Networks in Urban Quarters of Cairo* (Princeton, NJ: Princeton University Press, 1996), 269.

67 Bo Rothstein and Eric Uslaner, "All for All: Equality, Corruption, and Social Trust," *World Politics* 58 (2005): 41–72.

68 Robert Putnam, *Making Democracy Work: Civic Tradition in Modern Italy* (Princeton, NJ: Princeton University Press, 1993), 167.

69 William Mishler and Richard Rose, "What Are the Origins of Political Trust? Testing Institutional and Cultural Theories in Post-communist Societies," *Comparative Political Studies* 34, no. 1 (2001): 30–62.

70 Amaney Jamal, "When Is Social Trust a Desirable Outcome? Examining Levels of Trust in the Arab World," *Comparative Political Studies* 40, no. 11 (2007): 1328–1349.

71 Singerman, *Avenues of Participation*.

72 Emanuele Ferragina and Alessandro Arrigoni, "The Rise and Fall of Social Capital: Requiem for a Theory?," *Political Studies Review* 15, no. 3 (2017): 355–367.

73 For more discussions on the relation between trust and authoritarianism, see Jamal, "When Is Social Trust a Desirable Outcome?"

CHAPTER 6. DILEMMAS OF PARTICIPATION AND NONPARTICIPATION IN THE MENA REGION

1 Emma Murphy, "The In-securitisation of Youth in the South and East Mediterranean," *International Spectator* 53, no. 2 (2018): 21–37.

2 Lisa Wedeen, *Authoritarian Apprehensions: Ideology, Judgment, and Mourning in Syria* (Chicago: University of Chicago Press, 2019), 20.

3 Mayssoun Sukarieh and Stuart Tannock, *Youth Rising? The Politics of Youth in the Global Economy* (London: Routledge, 2015).

4 The sampling approach was not identical in all of them, but the results are representative at the national level. The sample in Palestine was composed of 1,353 individuals and was carried out from October 13, 2015, to December 31, 2015. In Morocco, the survey was carried out from December 14, 2015, until January 9,

2016, and included 1,022 young people. In Turkey, 1,804 young people were surveyed. For more discussions on research methodology, see Åge Tiltnes, http://power2youth.iai.it/survey.html.

5 Robert Springborg, "Globalization and Its Discontents in the MENA Region," *Middle East Policy* (Summer 2016): 146–160.

6 Adam Hanieh, *Lineages of Revolt* (Chicago: Haymarket Books, 2013).

7 Hanieh, *Lineages of Revolt*; Ishak Diwan, *Understanding the Political Economy of Arab Uprisings* (Hackensack, NJ: World Scientific Publishing, 2014).

8 Clement Henry and Robert Springborg, *Globalization and Political Development in the Middle East*, 2nd ed. (Cambridge: Cambridge University Press, 2010).

9 See, for instance, Oliver Schlumberger, "Structural Reform, Economic Order and Patrimonial Capitalism," *Review of International Political Economy* 15, no. 4 (2008): 622–649; Samer Soliman, *Autumn of Dictatorship: Fiscal Crisis and Political Change in Egypt under Mubarak* (Stanford, CA: Stanford University Press, 2011); Amaney Jamal, *Barriers to Democracy: The Other Side of Social Capital in Palestine and the Arab World* (Princeton, NJ: Princeton University Press, 2007); Diwan, *Understanding the Political Economy of Arab Uprisings*; Maha Abdelrahman, "Policing Neoliberalism in Egypt: The Continuing Rise of the 'Securocratic' State," *Third World Quarterly* 38, no. 1 (2017): 185–202; Angela Joya, "Neoliberalism, the State and Economic Policy Outcomes in the Post-Arab Uprisings: The Case of Egypt," *Mediterranean Politics* 22, no. 3 (2017): 339–361.

10 Hanieh, *Lineages of Revolt*.

11 Ibid., 65.

12 Nadine Sika, "Civil Society and the Rise of Unconventional Modes of Youth Participation in the MENA," *Middle East Law and Governance* 10, no. 3 (2018): 237–263.

13 See Jamal, *Barriers to Democracy*.

14 Abeer Musleh, "The Shortfall of Development Policies to Address Youth Issues in Palestine," Power2Youth working paper no. 11 (May 23, 2016), http://power2youth .iai.it/publications/the-shortfall-of-development-policies-to-address-youth-issues -in-palestine.html (accessed July 5, 2018).

15 Ibid.

16 Birzeit University, "Organizational Factors of Youth Exclusion in the Occupied Palestinian Territories," Power2Youth working paper no. 22 (December 9, 2016), http://power2youth.iai.it/publications/organizational-factors-of-youth-exclusion -and-inclusion-in-the-occupied-palestinian-territories.html (accessed July 5, 2018).

17 Ibid.

18 Ibid.

19 Ali Alper Akyüz, Gümüş Pınar, Volkan Yılmaz, and Ferhat Mahir Çakaloz, "Youth Exclusion and the Transformative Impact of Organized Youth in Turkey," Power2Youth working paper no. 21 (October 26, 2016), http://power2youth.iai.it /system/resources/

W1siZiIsIjIwMTYvMTAvMjYvMDlfNDNfMzRfODc4X3AyeV8yMS5wZGYiXV0
/p2y_21.pdf (accessed July 22, 2018).

20 Saloua Zerhouni and Azeddine Akesbi, "Youth Activism in Morocco: Exclusion,
Agency and the Search for Inclusion," Power2Youth working paper no. 15
(September 2016), www.iai.it/sites/default/files/p2y_15.pdf (accessed July 22,
2018), p. 10.

21 Mona Harb, "Youth Mobilization in Lebanon: Navigating Exclusion and Seeds for
Collective Action," Power2Youth working paper no. 16 (October 3, 2016), http://
power2youth.iai.it/publications/youth-mobilisation-in-lebanon-navigating-exclu
sion-and-seeds-for-collective-action.html (accessed July 1, 2018); Paul Kingston,
*Reproducing Sectarianism: Advocacy Networks and the Politics of Civil Society in
Postwar Lebanon* (Albany: State University of New York Press, 2013).

22 Janine Clark and Marie-Joëlle Zahar, "Critical Junctures and Missed
Opportunities: The Case of Lebanon's Cedar Revolution," *Ethnopolitics* 14, no. 1
(2015): 1–18; Harb, "Youth Mobilization in Lebanon."

23 Bassel Saloukh, Rabie Barakat, Jinan Al-Habbal, Lara Khattab, and Mikaelian
Shoghig, *The Politics of Sectarianism in Postwar Lebanon* (London: Pluto Press,
2015); Harb, "Youth Mobilization in Lebanon."

24 Harb, "Youth Mobilization in Lebanon."

25 Ibid.

26 Akyüz et al., "Youth Exclusion."

27 Ibid.

28 Zerhouni and Akesbi, "Youth Activism in Morocco"; Birzeit University,
"Organizational Factors of Youth Exclusion"; Akyüz et al., "Youth Exclusion";
Hassan Boubakri and Asma Bouzidi, "Tunisian Youth, from Obedience to
Protest," unpublished report (Rome: IAI, 2016); Saloukh et al., *Politics of
Sectarianism in Postwar Lebanon.*

29 Zerhouni and Akesbi, "Youth Activism in Morocco"; Mohammed Masbah,
"Moving towards Political Participation: The Moderation of Moroccan Salafis
since the Beginning of the Arab Spring," *SWP Comments*, no. 1 (January 2013),
www.swp-berlin.org/fileadmin/contents/products/comments/2013C01
_msb.pdf.

30 Akyüz et al., "Youth Exclusion."

31 Ibid.

32 Ibid., 17.

33 Boubakri and Bouzidi, "Tunisian Youth."

34 Ibid., 27.

35 Akyüz et al., "Youth Exclusion."

36 Tahir Abbas and Ismail Hakki Yigit, "Scenes from Gezi Park: Localisation,
Nationalism and Globalisation in Turkey," *City: Analysis of Urban Change, Theory,
Action* 19, no. 1 (2015): 61–76.

37 Erbatur Çavuşoğlu and Julia Strutz, "Producing Force and Consent: Urban Transformation and Corporatism in Turkey," *City: Analysis of Urban Change, Theory, Action* 18, no. 2 (2014): 134–148.
38 Akyüz et al., "Youth Exclusion."
39 Harb, "Youth Mobilization in Lebanon."
40 Zerhouni and Akesbi, "Youth Activism in Morocco."
41 Ibid.
42 Ibid.
43 For more information on the Polisario front, see www.britannica.com/topic/Polisario-Front.
44 Maria Cristina Paciello, Renata Pepicelli, and Daniela Pioppi, "Public Action towards Youth in Neo-liberal Morocco," Power2Youth working paper no. 5 (February 2016), www.iai.it/sites/default/files/p2y_05.pdf (accessed May 22, 2018).
45 See the movements' campaigns at www.stopthewall.org/the-wall.
46 *Palestine Chronicle*, "The Palestine Chronicle: The Authentic Voice of Palestine" (May 2018), www.birzeit.edu/en/news/al-wafaa-islamic-bloc-secures-majority-birzeit-university-student-council-elections (accessed July 2018).
47 Birzeit University, "Organizational Factors of Youth Exclusion."
48 Ibid.
49 *Middle East Eye*, "Palestinians React with Shock at PA Repression of Protest in Solidarity with Gaza" (June 14, 2018), www.middleeasteye.net (accessed July 10, 2018).
50 Harb, "Youth Mobilization in Lebanon."
51 Akyüz et al., "Youth Exclusion."
52 Murphy, "In-securitisation of Youth," 22. Emphasis in the original.
53 International Labour Organization (ILO), *Global Employment Trends for Youth 2017: Paths to a Better Working Future* (Geneva: ILO, 2017).
54 World Bank, Data Bank (2018), online at https://data.worldbank.org/.
55 Murphy, "In-securitisation of Youth."
56 Ibid.
57 Ibid., 30.
58 Ibid.
59 Ibid.
60 Jörg Gertel and Ralf Hexel, eds., *Coping with Uncertainty: Youth in the Middle East and North Africa* (London: Saqi, 2018).
61 Ibid., 160.
62 Maria Cristina Paciello et al., "Youth in Tunisia: Trapped between Public Control and the Neo-liberal Economy," Power2Youth working paper no. 6 (February 2016), http://power2youth.iai.it/system/resourcesW1siZiIsIjIwMTYvMDMvMD kvMTFfMzdfMDFfOTk1X3AyeV8wNi5wZGYiXVo/p2y_06.pdf, p. 10 (accessed May 22, 2018).

63 Zerhouni and Akesbi, "Youth Activism in Morocco."
64 Gertel and Hexel, *Coping with Uncertainty.*
65 Boubakri and Bouzidi, "Tunisian Youth"; Akyüz et al., "Youth Exclusion."
66 Akyüz et al., "Youth Exclusion."
67 Nadine Sika, "Varieties of Youth Civic and Political Engagement in the South East of the Mediterranean: A Comparative Analysis," working paper no. 23 (2017), www.iai.it/sites/default/files/p2y_23.pdf.
68 Zerhouni and Akesbi, "Youth Activism in Morocco."
69 Paciello et al., "Youth in Tunisia."
70 Murphy, "In-securitisation of Youth," 32.
71 Harb, "Youth Mobilization in Lebanon."
72 Birzeit University, "Organizational Factors of Youth Exclusion."

CONCLUSION

1 James Côté, "Towards a New Political Economy of Youth," *Journal of Youth Studies* 17, no. 4 (2014): 527–543.
2 Mayssoun Sukarieh and Stuart Tannock, "On the Political Economy of Youth: A Comment," *Journal of Youth Studies* 19, no. 9 (2016): 1281–1289.
3 Bruce Rutherford, "Egypt's New Authoritarianism under Sisi," *Middle East Journal* 72, no. 2 (Spring 2018): 185–208.
4 The percentages of military governors during Mubarak and al-Sisi are from Rutherford, "Egypt's New Authoritarianism under Sisi," while the percentage during Sadat's rule is from Zeinab Abul-Magd, "Egypt's Adaptable Officers: Business, Nationalism, and Dissent," in *Businessmen in Arms: How the Military and Other Armed Groups Profit in the MENA Region*, ed. Elke Grawert and Zeinab Abul-Magd (Lanham, MD: Rowman and Littlefield, 2016).
5 Joseph Demartini, "Change Agents and Generational Relationships: A Reevaluation of Mannheim's Problem of Generations," *Social Forces* 65, no. 1 (1985): 1–16; Jane Pilcher, "Mannheim's Sociology of Generations: An Undervalued Legacy," *British Journal of Sociology* 45, no. 3 (1994): 481–495. See also Emma Murphy, "The In-securitisation of Youth in the South and East Mediterranean," *International Spectator* 53, no. 2 (2018): 21–37.
6 Murphy, "In-securitisation of Youth."
7 Mayssoun Sukarieh and Stuart Tannock, "The Positivity Imperative: A Critical Look at the 'New' Youth Development Movement," *Journal of Youth Studies* 14, no. 6 (2011): 675–691.
8 For more analysis on "exit, voice and loyalty," see Albert Hirschman, *Exit, Voice and Loyalty: Responses to Decline in Firms, Organizations, and States* (Cambridge, MA: Harvard University Press, 1970); and Albert Hirschman, "'Exit, Voice and Loyalty': Further Reflections and a Survey of Recent Contributions," *Milbank Memorial Fund Quarterly: Health and Society* 58, no. 3 (1980): 430–453.
9 Murphy, "In-securitisation of Youth."

10 See Freedom House, "Freedom in the World: 2018," https://freedomhouse.org /report/freedom-world/2018/lebanon (accessed July 25, 2018).

11 See, for instance, Jan Jämte and Rune Ellefsen, "The Consequences of Soft Repression," *Mobilization: An International Journal* 25, no. 3 (2020): 383–404.

12 Côté, "Towards a New Political Economy of Youth."

INDEX

Page numbers in italics indicate Tables

February 20th youth movement, 139–40
feminism, 73–76
Freedom and Justice Party (FJP), 49
Free Egyptians' Party, political party, 73, 177n52
Free Officers movement, 13, 17; 1952 coup d'état, 34–35, 38
Free Student Union, 46
Friday of Anger, 80
Future Generation Foundation, 46, 57

gender struggles: in civic and political engagement, 73–76; in MENA, 76; NGOs as arena, 73–75; virginity testing, 75
Gezi Park demonstration, 136, 148–49
graffiti: as political activism, 90–91; against SCAF, 90; of UWK, 90

health insurance: in Lebanon, 144, *145*; for marginalized youth, 116; in Morocco, *116*
High Council of Universities, 50
al-Hirak movement, 138–39, 141, 156
hope: in civic and political engagement, 60–63; youth as hope of nation, 6–7, 14, 65, 70–71, 153; youth as threat and hope dilemma, 52–54, 153
human rights, 89, 92; founding of organizations, 155; movements, 101
Hussein, Saddam, 23

IFIs. *See* international financial institutions
IMF. *See* International Monetary Fund
Import Substitution and Industrialization model (ISI), 1, 16, 152
infitah: November 1968 intifada, 39; Sadat and, 18–22
International Conference on Population and Development, 42
international financial institutions (IFIs), 58, 64; depoliticization supported by, 70; privatization supported by, 128

International Monetary Fund (IMF), 19, 23, 58–59
Internet: confidence in, 124; NDP forums, 47; political activists and, 85, *85*. *See also* blogging; social media
intifada: Al-Aqsa intifada, 43; intifada of thieves, 41
ISI. *See* Import Substitution and Industrialization model
Islamic Jihad, 24
Islamists, 134, 136; Freedom and Justice Party, 49; student movements, 40–41
Israel: 1967 war with Egypt, 38–39; peace with, 19, 24

January 25 uprising, 48–49, 101
June 2013 demonstrations, 67, 72, 100
Justice and Development Party (AKP), 11; opposition to, 136, 138; youth wing of, 134

Kadet al-Mustaqbal, 69
Kifaya movement, 43–44

labor: growth in labor migration, 19; labor movements, 88, 102; market rigidities, 117
Law 32, 28
Law 84, 28, 59
Law of Shame, 21
Lebanon, 128, 156; health insurance in, 144, *145*; al-Hirak movement, 138–39, 141; NGOs in, 133; #YouStink movement, 138–39
Liberals, 40
loyalty: Sadat and loyal opposition, 40; youth as, 8–9, 79

Mada Masr, 65
Al-Mahala workers strike, 44
Mansour, Adly, 29, 30, 51, 52

MENA youth, 128–29, 143–44, 146; rise
of, 105–7; youth precarities and, 143
Power2Youth project (P2Y), 57, 60, 71, 112,
128, 142, 147, 156
privatization, 168n73; IFIs supporting,
128; under Mubarak, H., 25–26
protection pact with elite, 152
protests, 3, 10, 65; Arab Spring, 141; Arab
uprisings, 10, 27, 88, 139; February 20th
youth movement, 139–40; January 25
uprising, 48–49, 101; Ministry of Interior approving, 52; in OPT, 136, 137, 140;
protest law of 2013, 52; Rab'a Massacre,
90, 100, 174n87; SCAF banning, 105;
social media and, 138; Students against
the Coup group, 90; Tahrir Square sit-
in (1972), 40, 43, 75, 80; in Tunisia, 136,
137; of university activists, 92–94; Youth
for Change movement, 44, 87–88. See
also demonstrations; infitah; intifada;
riots; strikes
provision pact with elite, 152

qualitative analysis, 12, 57, 128, 157, 164n54

Rab'a Massacre, 90, 100, 174n87
RCC. See Revolutionary Command Council
reform: civic and political engagement for,
76–78; education reform, 64; market-
oriented reforms, 157; market reforms,
117; for Ministry of Interior, 98; perceptions of MENA youth, 147–48; political
activism and, 98–100; SCAF and, 98
repression, 4, 152–53; activism-repression
nexus, 88–92; Mubarak, H., policies, 25, 27–29; of political activism,
37, 83–84; against poor, 29; against
university activists, 92–94
Republican Guard Massacre, 89
research methods, 12–14
Revolutionary Command Council
(RCC), 35–36

Revolutionary Socialists, 91
riots: bread riots (1977), 19, 41, 153; Nasr
Street riot, 89

Sabri, Ali, 17–18
Sadat, Anwar, 1, 17; assassination of, 20,
22; authoritarianism of, 2, 13; Corrective Revolution of, 18, 20; infitah and,
18–22; Law of Shame and, 21; loyal
opposition and, 40; market economy
and, 19–20; military and, 18, 152;
Ministry of Interior strengthened by,
18, 20, 33; political liberalization and,
20–21; youth in regime of, 39–42
Said, Khaled, 29
Salafi movement, 134–35
SCAF. See Supreme Council of the
Armed forces
securitization, 2, 70, 151; market economy
and, 152; perspective of youth, 5–7, 14;
political economy of youth and, 3; of
public sphere, 66–67
self-censorship, 92
self-policing, 92
Shabab Jabhet al-Inkaz, 86
shrinking of street, 66–67
Al-Sisi, Abdel Fattah, 12; civic and political engagement restricted by, 68–70,
78–79; consequences of political
activism strategies, 94–95; co-optation
by, 73; freedoms restricted by, 52; marginalization by, 72; market-oriented
reforms, 157; military and, 32, 152;
neoliberal economic model under, 32;
NGO law and, 30; political activism
viewed as threat, 101–2; political parties banned by, 60; regime benefits,
1–2; rise of, 29–32; strategies for political activism, 82–84; virginity testing
condoned, 75; youth in Egyptian
politics and, 51–54; youth strategies, 13
SKP. See Justice and Development Party

ABOUT THE AUTHOR

NADINE SIKA is Associate Professor of Comparative Politics at the American University in Cairo. She is the author of *Youth Activism and Contentious Politics in Egypt: Dynamics of Continuity and Change*; editor of *Dynamics of Youth Agency in Times of Crisis*; and co-editor with Eberhard Kienle of *The Arab Uprisings: Transforming and Challenging State Power*. Her recent articles appeared in journals such as *Democratization*, *Political Studies*, and *Mediterranean Politics*. She has been a recipient of various international grants from Humboldt Foundation, and Carnegie Corporation New York.